Sanctity and
Male Desire

Sanctity and Male Desire

A GAY READING OF SAINTS

Donald L. Boisvert

THE
PILGRIM
PRESS
Cleveland

For André (RIP),
Bernard (RIP),
David,
Brian,
and by no means least,
Ayman

The Pilgrim Press
700 Prospect Avenue
Cleveland, Ohio 44115-1100
thepilgrimpress.com

Printed in the United States of America on acid-free paper

09   08   07   06   05   04   5   4   3   2   1

Library of Congress Cataloging-in-Publication Data
Boisvert, Donald L., 1951- .
    Sanctity and male desire : a gay reading of saints / Donald L. Boisvert.
    p.   cm.
    Includes bibliographical references (p.   ) and index.
    ISBN 0-8298-1523-6 (paperback. : alk. paper)
    1. Christian saints. 2. Homosexuality – Religious aspects – Catholic
Church. 3. Desire – Religious aspects – Catholic Church. 4. Boisvert,
Donald L., 1951- 5. Religious biography.   I. Title.
BX4655.3.B67   2004
282′.092′2 – dc22
                                                            2004053495

Contents

Introduction

I WAS RAISED A CATHOLIC. At a time when the church was entering the difficult transition period heralded by the Second Vatican
Council, saints still played a very important role in my life, as they
did for most Catholic youth of that era. Not all saints, however. My
interest was with the male ones. They were my heroes and friends.
As I am gay, I believe they were also the earliest objects of my fantasies. I could admire these saints, love them from afar, want to be
like them, and also want to die like them. While other boys may have
been enthralled with sports stars or comic book figures, I was moved
by the iconic image of the masculine saint. I have never really lost
my fascination with saints. They still speak very powerfully to me of
human limitations transformed and made sacred and, most assuredly,
of erotic yearning.

As its title suggests, this is a book about how saints can instill desire.
I come at this topic as a gay scholar of religion. It is important for me
to state this at the start — not because I need to apologize (far from
it), but rather because this book constitutes a theological reflection
on my life experience. As such, it attempts to make sense of what has
been, for me, one of the formative aspects of my life *both* as a gay man
and as a scholar of religion: that of male sanctity. I further believe,
and I argue, that male sanctity has been a defining theme — very often
unacknowledged — in the lives of many Catholic gay men of my generation. These pages attempt to explore and hopefully explain the why
and the how. In some important ways, therefore, this book represents
an inquiry into the roots of contemporary gay Catholic culture.

Introduction

In his fascinating and insightful book, *The Silence of Sodom*, plainly subtitled *Homosexuality in Modern Catholicism*, Mark D. Jordan argues persuasively for a reading of Catholic clerical culture as both homoerotic and campy. His contention is that Roman Catholic theological discourse, through a series of deliberate rhetorical devices, effectively "silences" homosexuality within the church, while at the same time opening up a vast panoply of performative possibilities for its energetic expression in, among other places, Catholic liturgical and cultic life.[1] I believe male saints are very much a part of such "possibilities." Knowing full well that our emerging sexual yearnings for the bodies of other boys were totally unacceptable, I and other young Catholic boys were nonetheless encouraged to adore and worship — and by extension, to desire — the bodies of the saints, to say nothing of the half-naked crucified God himself. We were repeatedly taught to be chaste, but were pushed simultaneously into the welcoming arms of those virile holy men to whom we prayed. The male saint thus became an erotic fixation, an ever-present site of potential sexual affirmation and release. This was the stark manifestation of a Catholic culture at once repressive and liberating, of a Catholicism that bespoke homoerotic desire while also denying it vociferously. It was the Catholicism into which I was born and which I, like so many others of my generation, either had to learn to live within, or to transcend. Some of my generation of gay men did stay, choosing to accommodate ourselves silently; others could not, and left in large numbers.

I first had the inspiration for this book while attending an academic conference. Having just completed my first book, I was tossing about for a topic for a second one. I had listened to a paper exploring the popular image of the young Matthew Shepard as martyr. Several persons in the audience objected vehemently to such a characterization, claiming that it disempowered and marginalized gay men even further. Someone else suggested that, in fact, sanctity in the Catholic

tradition is very much an accessible and empowering model of behavior. This set me thinking about the saints of my youth, and how
they may have contributed, in some positive ways, to my sense of
self as a gay man and as a believer. This book is the result. It argues
that images of masculine sanctity can indeed be very powerful sites
for the emergence of a healthy and positive gay identity.

Queer Catholic Roots

I was raised in a household and in a culture where the cult of saints
held a place of honor. As the oldest male child of French Canadian
Catholic parents, who themselves were descendants of generations
of French Canadian Catholics come before, I was heir to a strong
legacy of religious fervor. Both my sets of grandparents, and especially my grandmothers (for when is religion not a women's thing?),
were intensely pious, as was my own mother. One of the most vivid
memories of my childhood is that of kneeling on my maternal grandmother's country kitchen floor, reciting the rosary which was being
broadcast live on the radio from the cathedral in Montreal. How I
hated it, in all my youthful restlessness! Yet I would continue, years
later, reciting the *paters* and the *aves* as a way of putting myself to
sleep when insomnia threatened to claim me in the wee hours of the
morning. Of my paternal grandmother, I recall that she was a kindly
but tough woman always dressed in black, whose bedroom walls were
covered with images of Jesus, Mary, and any number of very gaudy
Catholic-looking saints. She was always picking on my poor grandfather, who, like his sons, was known to enjoy putting back a few
and taking the Good Lord's name in vain. She reprimanded him, but
there was great and tender affection between them.

The saints who inhabited this ultramontane and ardent Catholic
world, some of whom would eventually become part of my psychic
and spiritual landscape, were ferociously popular and Gallic in their

appeal: Joseph, John the Baptist, Anthony, Francis, Louis, Jude, Ann, Joan of Arc, and of course, Thérèse of Lisieux. Above them all stood the Virgin Mary in her various avatars: Our Lady of Lourdes, of Fatima, of the Rosary, of the Seven Sorrows, of Charity, of Divine Help. Much devotion was centered around the Sacred Heart and the three figures of the Holy Family (Jesus, Mary, and Joseph), and I also recall that the child Jesus himself was a particularly popular and endearing figure of reverence. Two of my favorite statues as a child were a small one of the Holy Family and a larger plaster one of the kingly Infant of Prague, who had real clothes that I could touch and fondle. It was here that I learned how malleable and sensual my love affair with saints could be.

On some saints' feast-days, I would light vigil lamps in front of their statue as a means of honoring them, but also no doubt because it was a way for me as a child to engage in some sort of religious play. Contrary to the usual Catholic expectations with respect to the devotion of saints, I have never perceived or approached them as powers that could perform small favors, or that could intervene in some extraordinary way with the far more omnipotent Power. I do not recall praying to a particular saint for some cure or some hopeless cause, though I may have whispered a shy invocation to Saint Anthony upon losing some small personal memento. Praying to saints was never a big thing for me. I much preferred worshiping them from afar, for it was their heroic, almost superhuman stature that appealed to me. I wanted to keep my distance, because then it was easier to love and admire them. Their remoteness only served to fan my desires, in the same way that, years later, a particularly attractive or sexy man could drive me crazy simply by standing slightly above the mundane concerns of the everyday.

As Catholics of the 1950s and 1960s, we were all called to be saints. In our schools and churches, as well as in our devotional literature,

Introduction

the teachings were quite explicit: each one of us, in his or her life context, was expected to strive for and to attain sanctity. The unspoken
presumption was that, if we carefully followed the doctrines of Holy
Mother Church, then we would most assuredly attain, after death,
a state of saintly bliss and, who knew, perhaps the formal status of
the canonized saint. The models of sanctity being proposed were, of
course, theologically and morally correct in the extreme, but that
was the point. As good and loyal sons and daughters of the church,
we had to maintain orthodox obedience. Sainthood was therefore
a way for the nonclerical to achieve spiritual stature in an institution dominated by a heavily clerical view of reality. Though it could
certainly be a religiously empowering path for the laity, it nonetheless remained a canonically controlled one. Still, the call to sanctity
was there. One of its unspoken rules was the understanding that, if
you were under vows — either as a priest, nun, or brother — your
chances of attaining sainthood were significantly enhanced. One of
the comforting and attractive things about seminary life, which I entered when I was thirteen, was not only the fact that you were treated
as a priest-in-the-making, but, more importantly, as a potential saint.
We, of course, being typical adolescent boys, knew better in our rebellion. There certainly were no saints that I can recall among my
classmates.

It is no doubt ironic that one of the most homophobic and intol-
erant of religious institutions should have produced such an amazing
pantheon of attractive masculine holy figures. One of the great internal contradictions, and also one of the most attractive and enticing
qualities, of Roman Catholicism remains its remarkable ability to
negate the erotic while boldly affirming it in its art and rituals. This
is expressed most evidently in the central figure of Christ himself,
but it also finds strong echo in all those chaste bearded men or nubile
martyred youths who fill the ranks of its blessed. It has often been ob-
served that there are certain natural affinities between the pomp and

11

circumstance of the Church of Rome and the performative extravagance of gay culture. In many ways, male saints can be quite campy, despite their hypermasculinized or even sexless image. I would affirm that young Catholic gay boys growing up in a world without models to emulate would turn quite instinctively to these saints for a validation of their emerging sexual selves. As always, the line between the erotic and the religious is porous in the extreme.

Porous it certainly was for me. As a child, I collected holy cards and images of saints. I had statues of saints which I displayed on the makeshift altar in my bedroom, and I would play with them as one does with dolls or toy fire engines. There may have been some nascent erotic feeling at work here, though it never came through very clearly in my own mind. There was something arousing and tactile about these images and statues, however. As a young girl may learn some of the patterns and expectations of motherhood through her interaction with dolls, so I believe I was coming to an equally sharp sense of who and, more importantly, *what* I was through my fixation and relationships with male figures of sanctity. Who and what I have now become is due, in no small measure, to these early stirrings awakened in me by the ecstatic look of the transfigured and manly Catholic saint.

The Names of Desire

The saints in this book have been selected for a variety of reasons. First and most obviously, they are important to me in some way. They have all, at some point in my life, had an impact on me, from either a devotional or an intellectual perspective. In addition, they "represent" different forms of erotic yearning, and each embodies a particular image or quality of what masculinity may have meant to me, or still does. The life and spirituality of each is also different, so each carries a unique theological template. These saints have also been chosen because they are iconic, I believe, of what it might mean to be gay in the world today. In this sense, I suspect they are still very much actual and relevant, and I endeavor to discern and uncover what this might mean. There certainly is a homoerotic subtext — whether subtle or not — to Catholic male sainthood. This is how I choose to read it, and how I intend to state my case.

I begin with Michael the Archangel because he is more symbolic than real, and because his sculpted gladiatorial body was my earliest turn-on. He is followed by the early martyrs, most notably Saints Sebastian and Tarcisius, who occupy unique positions in Christian hagiography, and who touch upon issues of *eros* and *thanatos*. A series of very masculine saints comes after — John the Baptist, Joseph, Paul, and Augustine — each of whom has been more of a distant ideal than anything else, and at least two of whom have been problematic for gay men. These saints reflect my ambivalence toward institutionalized masculinity. They are followed by another series of martyrs, collective and more contemporary in this case — known as Ugandan and North American — who raise particular issues relating to the dynamics of desire and acculturation. The Christian saint *par excellence,* Francis of Assisi, is next. He is the very epitome of the social and religious rebel. I then turn to a very important saint in my early religious and sexual development, Dominic Savio. It is here that I discuss the only female figure in the book, Saint Maria Goretti, through the eyes of her male murderer. Blessed Damien of Molokai and some other missionary saints follow. In their imperialistic self-lessness, they represented a certain altruistic ideal for me. The last figure is Saint Peter Julian Eymard, not an especially well-known saint, but one who is important to me because of his unique role as my religious mentor and father. The two final chapters look at the figure of Christ, the manliest of all manly saints, and at certain gay individuals as hagiographic figures. In my conclusion, I reflect briefly upon the imagery and lives of two other saints — John the Evangelist and Thomas More — in terms of the gay iconography of "lover" and "activist."

I should say a brief word about God-language. As is common practice, I would normally use gender-inclusive language when referring to the divine. In several passages in this book, however, I do refer to God in the masculine. I have done so for two reasons. First, this is a book written by a gay man about male desire as it relates to male saints. My frame of reference in writing was masculine, and I have tried consciously to remain within it, even when naming or gendering the godhead. Second, in those chapters that explore such issues as fatherhood or the figure of the erotic Christ, for example, it seemed more logical and consistent to refer to God as masculine, which is why I have opted to do so. I do not mean to imply, of course, that God is a man, but rather that my paradigms for understanding the issues raised in the book take their cue from my own gender and sexual orientation.

Some Protestants may puzzle at having a chapter devoted to Jesus because they view him as savior rather than saint. But the Latin word *Sanctus* simply means "holy," and in Catholic traditions Jesus is viewed as the supreme source of all holiness. He is "holy (or saint) savior." Those not familiar with the long tradition of devotion to the saints may also not be aware of the extreme earthiness of this devotion. The descriptive words and phrases used in this book are in line with a tradition that has emphasized the humanness of holy persons and the sensualism of our response to them.

Searching for a Gay Hagiography

In some ways, this book is a preliminary attempt at crafting a gay hagiography. I mean this in a dual sense: first, as the search for a gay interpretation of traditionally Catholic images of sanctity; and second, as a unique hagiographic "take" on gay icons and personages.

14

Hagiography refers simply to "the writing of saints' lives."[2] While I do not attempt to write the lives of my chosen saints, I certainly reinterpret them in unusual ways. Perhaps, therefore, my effort is more consistent with a certain form of hagiology, that is, "literature treating of lives and legends of saints." The word "legend" is revealing. There can be no doubt that much of what we choose to ascribe to certain saints belongs properly to the domain of symbol and invention. In fact, I would think that a significant portion of a given saint's attractiveness rests with the stories and folklore that surround his or her persona. Mine may therefore be more of a literary enterprise than a strictly theological one. As such, I claim, of necessity, the imaginative freedom of the literary writer, though it may force me to engage in a bit of hagiolatry at times.

The study of saints is not an esoteric subgenre of some bizarre field of research, though it can certainly turn into that, as it has at certain times in history. It does have very distinguished scholarly foundations. As a rule, contemporary studies of sainthood and sanctity highlight the sociological and cultural roles of saint-making and of the individual saint.[3] I follow this approach. In discussing these saints, I opt for different levels of analysis. First, I look at their lives and the symbolic discourse that surrounds them. This is the most purely hagiographic part of the investigation. Second, I try to connect this biographical exploration with some sense of what the saint *represents* as a kind of social or cultural construct. Third, I engage in a process of critical self-reflection, placing the saint and his image in the context of my development and identity as a gay man. Fourth, I extrapolate from this onto gay culture as a whole, sketching the parameters of what the saint might mean as a gay symbol or figure. Throughout, however, I affirm that sanctity *is* a form of cultural discourse and meaning, and that the only truly valid way of apprehending sanctity is through an assertion of its socially charged iconographic power. The saint, in other words, *represents* something.

I have chosen to write exclusively about male saints because I am exploring male sanctity. In doing so, I have, of course, deliberately "gendered" my hagiography. I do not wish to be dismissive of female sanctity. What, if anything, do I need to say at this point about it? Is there something that distinguishes female from male sanctity, and which might further inform and enrich my study? I would suggest, without great surprise, that the two types of sanctity are reflective of the relative historical positioning of the sexes. In both cases, however, sanctity could also be a worthy path to the attainment of cultural and sexual power — perhaps more so for women, of necessity, than for men. Models of sanctity for women, particularly those centered on the religious or conventual life, made possible the development of certain life options clearly removed from the orbit and dominance of male influence and power. Including the figure of Mary herself, female saints in the Catholic tradition tend to reflect the church's own sexist view of women. Female saints are predominantly virgins or consecrated women (or reformed whores, as is often supposed in the case of Mary Magdalene), and the vast majority of them appear to have been more than fleetingly preoccupied with intense bodily discipline as a sure means to spiritual enlightenment. Though male saints also engaged in episodes of extreme physical mortification, theirs was couched more in the rhetoric of hypermasculine fortitude. In fact, male saints, precisely because they inhabited masculine bodies, never had to view and control their sexuality in quite the same dramatic way as was expected of female saints, who, because they were women, were seen as tainted and weak from the start.

Female saints have always been rather distant and foreign, if at all present, in my fantastical world of religious heroes. They have never resonated with me in quite the same way that their male counterparts have. The exceptions are few: Saint Ann, the mother of Mary and an important saint in the religious history of Quebec; Saint Clare of Assisi, because of her association with Francis; Saint Thérèse of Lisieux, arguably the most popular saint of the last century; and Saint Maria Goretti. What the experience of a Catholic lesbian of my generation might be regarding female saints would certainly be very interesting to explore. Models of female sanctity, for me, have generally been associated with nuns and martyred virgins, with founders of religious congregations and holy widows: all legitimate professional choices for women, but none of which sparked my religious imagination. Give me the male saint, however, that paragon of manly and powerful religious desire, and I would go quite weak at the knees. No doubt this was a reflection of my perception of the relative social positioning of males, including myself, but it was also the expression of youthful sexual desire. All of which simply goes to show, once again, the very close affinities between our nascent erotic yearnings and our religious ones, and the necessary conflation of the two.

Hagiography is a constantly changing form of religious and cultural discourse. One of the more intriguing and creative things about saints is their adaptability to place and time. Each generation can choose to reinterpret them in light of its own values and concerns. What I am doing here is no different. I come to my topic from the perspective of a gay man at the dawn of the twenty-first century. As such, I choose to see my saints as somehow relevant to contemporary gay culture. This requires an imaginative leap. It is, however, a necessary leap, for only by doing so can we hope to contribute to the elaboration of a relevant gay spirituality in this day and age. There is, in my estimation, no more compelling or necessary task for the gay scholar of religion.

Sanctity, Sensuality, and Popular Religiosity

Saints represent one of the most accessible forms of religion. In Catholic culture, saints stand as privileged intermediaries between humans and the divine. They can intercede for us, granting special favors and cures, helping us to overcome the large and small obstacles of our lives. They are also considered models of human perfection, exemplary and inspirational in their lives and accomplishments, which is why all Catholics are called to sanctity. The veneration of saints reflects much about how people view and apprehend the sacred, and how they choose to define themselves in relation to it. Saints, after all, were once real people. Because of this, they are considerably easier to relate to in a meaningful way than the somewhat distant and powerful figure of God. We can establish personal relationships with saints, and the old story of the saint's statue being placed face to the wall because he or she failed to come through on some request is very telling in this regard. We feel we can punish saints for failing us as intercessors, even though they are ultimately seen as being repositories of divine grace and power. We fear them, while still treating them like children. We revere them, but we never really forget that they were once subject to the same human foibles and needs as us.

Saints perform a dual role of mediation and model. They are at once intercessory and exemplary. We can model our lives on those of the saints. We know how they lived and died, and the kinds of sufferings and obstacles they had to overcome. Saints are also heroic. They teach us that mundane existence can be glorified, and that it is very much possible to surmount and transcend human contingency. In this sense, saints, while still remaining intensely human, become almost superhuman. They make it possible for us — indeed, they challenge us — to be the same as them. This notion of heroism was central to my own appreciation of saints in my youth. It framed my religious and social experience as a Catholic boy, spurring me on to heights of adulatory self-control and piety, and providing me with a context within which it all somehow made sense. If my hero was the saint, then I had to be as larger-than-life as he was. I also had to attain a similar state of heroic perfection. I had to learn to control my sexual feelings and my fluttering hunger for the touch of other boys, as the saints themselves controlled their myriad of strong and obsessive urges.

Saints are sensual beings, and the forms of piety that they elicit can be equally sensual, and sometimes even sexual, in form and content. Anyone who has had the opportunity to observe the veneration of saints' statues in intensely Catholic cultures — such as Latin ones, for example — is struck almost immediately by the care and attention heaped upon them. They are clothed and bathed, covered with flowers or dripping in bright red droplets of blood, gaudy and almost comical in their painted features, and lit by the reflective glow of a thousand votive candles. Religious icons or holy figures in any religion — whether East or West — are treated in the same way. Saints are like adult dolls. We love to play with them, feel them, dress them up, and display them. Their graven figures and imagined bodies become amulets, protecting us against the more frightening parts of our nature — and sometimes, those of others. Perhaps they really are inspired copies of us, performative extensions of who we think we should be at our best moments.

Sociologists of religion like to point to the cult of saints as one of the more telling examples of the persistence and appeal of popular religion. There is a great deal of truth to this. In Roman Catholicism, the cult of saints has been widespread while still being perceived, at times, as defiantly subversive of formal orthodoxy: a parallel theological and devotional discourse, as it were, to that of the church hierarchy. This is an intriguing aspect of the dynamics of sainthood. It underscores the particular quality of the cult of saints in challenging established social conventions. Some scholars have highlighted the unique role of devotion to certain saints as a means of "acquiring power" for those who may be culturally marginal.[4] Interestingly enough, though excessive devotion to saints may sometimes make the Catholic Church anxious, no other pope has canonized so many saints during his pontificate as John Paul II. This fact eloquently demonstrates the indispensability of tactile and sensual religiosity in ultimately shoring up the often shifting and increasingly discredited foundations of institutionalized belief.

My saints are tactile and sensual, and their bodies, real or imagined, play a significant part in this book, as they have in my religious and erotic life. My saints are the men of my dreams. They are the companions of my imaginary voyages and of my quest for spiritual fulfillment. There can be no doubt that these saints circumscribed my earliest attempts at making sense of the Catholicism in which I grew up: a Catholicism marked by an obsession with ritual and imagery, and which I still so desperately miss at times. My saints were my earliest spiritual friends and mentors, the very real embodiment of what I thought it meant to be a committed believer. In this sense, they were true religious icons and symbols. When I was picked on by my playmates for whatever reason (usually because I couldn't throw a ball or do similar boyish things), I could transform myself into the Roman martyr persecuted by his tormentors. When I thought of escaping the dullness of my adolescent existence, I could dream of being a missionary in some far-flung part of the earth, ministering to exotic and dangerous natives. Saints were a way of asserting my solitude and my difference, and of somehow ennobling them with a more just and cohesive purpose. I suspect most gay boys develop similar strategies of their own for coping with their isolation. They model their behavior and reactions on what they think are more appealing and meaningful exemplars of masculinity, whether these be their fathers or brothers, or the heroes and tough guys of the movies and cartoons. It just so happened that my choices were more religious and perhaps a bit more unusual than most.

A final image of saints dominates my mind. It is that of my mother dying from cancer, and of the relics and images of two saints she had pinned to her clothes. She was young, in her late thirties. These amulets did not save her, but they remain engraved in my memory. There were three relics. The first was a small circular picture of the Sacred Heart. The second, containing a piece of cloth that had touched the body of the holy one, was of Blessed Marie-Rose Durocher, the foundress of an order of French Canadian teaching sisters, and to which one of my great-aunts belonged. The third was a relic of Saint Peter Julian Eymard, the founder of the religious congregation whose seminary I was to enter in a few months, and about which my mother was so proud. The thing that strikes me most about this eclectic duo of saints is how personal it was to my mother: one relic linking her to her own immediate family, in the guise of her aunt's spiritual mother; the other, a symbolic tie to the saint to whom she was about to offer her firstborn son. In many ways, this beautifully expresses the real meaning of the devotion to saints. While my mother was no doubt hoping (perhaps against hope itself) that these images and relics held some curative power, she was also affirming, in her suffering body, the ties that still bound her to the living. Ultimately, this is what saints do. They reaffirm our common humanity, and they link us, not only with each other, but also with the ineffably Other.

This, then, is a love story between a Catholic gay boy growing up in mid-twentieth-century North America and Saint Dominic Savio, Saint Joseph, Saint Francis, Saint Peter Julian Eymard, and some others among the masculine heavenly host. It is a curious tale of sexual discovery and religious zeal. It is, in the end, a book about desire, as all books should be.

I embark on this writing in a spirit of excitement and gratitude: excitement because it remains largely uncharted territory, and gratitude because I am really giving myself a chance to delve into one of my true lifelong obsessions. May all the saints of heaven — but especially the men — be by my side as I forge ahead in my rather daunting quest. May they grant me discernment and courage.

Parts of chapters 7, 8, 10, and 12 were given in September 2002 as talks for an MCC conference on spirituality and sexuality on a cruise ship from California to Mexico. I am most grateful to the organizers, and particularly the Reverend Justin Tanis, for this unique opportunity, but also for the sheer fun of it all. In addition, some of the text in chapter 10 originally appeared in *White Crane Journal*, no. 55 (Winter 2002).

Sincere thanks are once again expressed to the publisher at The Pilgrim Press, Timothy G. Staveteig, and to my former editor, George R. Graham, for their willingness to work with a somewhat unorthodox text. To my current editor, Pamela J. Johnson, I say thank you for the care and support, and for her gentleness with the red pencil. I am also much obliged to Paul J. Gorrell for his inspired comment on Matthew Shepard and saints, which got me thinking about all this in the first place; to Robert Pinet who, while talking about possible sexual escapades over brunch one Boxing Day, helped me see something about top and bottom saints; and to my long-standing and dear friend John Skates for the timely reference to the nude Christ on the Barcelona Sagrada Familia. For Brian, I'm glad you were there at the very beginning, and I'm sorry I forgot to mention it the first time 'round. One could not ask for a more perfect mentor. And to Gaston, my anchor, as always, *merci.*

Sanctity and
Male Desire

ONE

Michael the Archangel

W HEN I WAS IN THE SEMINARY, the chapel attached to our study
quarters was called Saint Michael's. Above the front doors in an
alcove stood an immense statue of the archangel. Because there was
a side door leading to the chapel from inside the school, we seldom
entered through the front. When we did, however, I would always
look up at Saint Michael. In doing so, I invariably found myself staring up his short skirt. There wasn't much to see, though many were
the times that my pubescent hopes outstripped reality. I do remember I found it odd that there was not even a pair of ironware briefs
on the angel. There was nothing: simply a mass of metal. The fun-
niest thing about looking up inside the statue, however, was seeing
that hornets had built a nest along the edge of the skirt. Somehow,
its texture and shape meshed quite perfectly with those of the statue.
Though the statue itself, much to our disappointment, may not have
contained any symbol of regenerative capacity, life in the form of in-
sects was certainly teeming and humming where the angel's mighty
sexual organs should have been.

All in bronze, Michael was truly colossal. I remember that he had
big, broad shoulders and huge, sturdy legs. The face somehow escapes
me, but I do recall that he had curly hair. He was dressed in the typical military attire of the Roman soldier, the manner in which he is
always portrayed, with his wings tightly wound up round his sides.
He was very masculine, and if I had known then what I know now,
I would have said that the sculptor was gay. There was ruggedness

and a disarming charm about him. It was almost as though Michael were standing guard over our young lives with his protruding sword and his fatherlike gaze, ever ready to gather us in times of trouble and doubt under his massive wings. I am quite sure that I was not the only seminarian who found Michael to his liking. Not doubt many others had passed under the statue and stared up expectantly, hoping that Michael's skirt would come alive and fluff in the wind, revealing some truly unspeakable wonders and delights.

Actually, as seminarians we spent a great deal of time hoping to catch a glimpse of what could be found under clothes — or at least, I did. We had many opportunities to do so: in the dormitories, the locker rooms, or sometimes simply while daydreaming in class. And then, of course, there were the shower rooms, when so very little was left to the imagination. In such cases, what was before our eyes often far surpassed the wild images of our overheated minds. For a gay boy, seminary life was all about sideways glances and lowered eyes. Though there certainly was a sharp and delightful thrill in seeing your classmates naked, you had to be careful not to let your look linger lest you be pegged as the school sissy boy. So, as homosexuals have down through the ages, you learned discretion, and subtlety, and a thousand and one tricks for indulging in the stolen peek. You had to in order to survive.

My expectation at seeing underwear on Michael's statue had more to do with the image of a particularly well-built and well-endowed upperclassmate standing by his bed in his white cotton jockeys. A true specimen of manliness, this classmate was the son of a military family and was later to serve and, as I recall, die in Vietnam. He was sweet and gentle, and he took a liking to me. Nothing ever happened between us. Our relationship was more that of an older brother to a younger child, or one between favorite cousins. But this picture of his finely sculpted body clad only in briefs remains one of the more vivid of my years in minor seminary. I was so enthralled with his physique that I would try to take my morning shower at the same time as him, simply to gaze at his erect nakedness. He was a warrior. We all knew that he wanted to fight "over there" as a member of the Green Berets, but this, despite my more liberal antiwar feelings, only made him more desirable in my youthful eyes. To my unconscious mind, perhaps he and Michael the Archangel were really one and the same, and perhaps my staring up the latter's tunic was really a means of expressing my frustration at not being able to get my hands on that impeccably white and unattainable pair of jockeys.

Tradition has it that Saint Michael fought against the forces of the angel Lucifer at the beginning of the world, when the latter rose up in rebellion against God and was flung into the eternal fires of hell after the primeval battle between good and evil. Because of this, Michael has always been cast in the guise of a warrior, and customary images show him standing proudly and triumphantly on top of a dragon — the devil himself — with victorious spear or sword in hand. He is always handsome. Some traditions maintain that Michael was the angel sent to drive Adam and Eve from the Garden of Eden, and that he was also the one who guided the Israelites through the desert. In conventional Catholic teaching, he is seen as the fearless defender of the church against the forces of a heretical world. Saint Michael the Archangel has always been characterized as a protector of what is right, just, and good. In fact, he has been used time and again as a staunchly conservative symbol of defense against the apparently corrosive evils of liberalism and communism.[5] Before the revision of the church's calendar of saints in the 1970s, he shared his feast day, September 29, with the two other important angelic figures of the Bible: Gabriel and Raphael, messenger and guide, respectively. This day now belongs not to the three archangels, whose existence can't really be proven, but to a series of minor and far more prosaic Blesseds, thereby demonstrating how far the mighty can sometimes fall. Michael, who no longer officially has a feast day of his own, is also one of the few saints shared by different religious traditions, a sort of ecumenical go-between. He is God's right-hand man, the one who gets the job done and who always does it so well.

As an angel, Saint Michael is, of course, a spirit. Strictly speaking, no one really knows what he looks like, though one can always argue about how many of his angelic companions can dance on the head of a pin, as medieval theologians were so fond of asking. It is therefore possible to picture him as we see fit. Angelic creatures are usually portrayed as either female or as highly androgynous. Images show them as soft, slightly vaporous beings. They are usually clothed in flowing pink or powder-blue pastel robes. Michael, on the other hand, is a military man, a gladiator, a born fighter. In Catholic tradition, he is also the patron saint of policemen, a highly masculinized and violent profession. One is struck, however, by the almost contradictory way in which his face is depicted. At times, he has the sexually ambivalent look typical of angels; at others, he resembles a modern athlete, that paragon of manly energy and charisma. There is an inherent ambivalence to the figure of Michael: he is either very masculine-looking or he is genderless (or perhaps even bisexual, depending on your perspective). The defender of the Catholic Church is therefore a sexually uncertain creature. This is highly symbolic, I would argue, of the church's discourse on eroticism generally — a discourse which, while claiming to be clearly unambiguous in its defense of gender roles, nonetheless harbors a strangely flirtatious pull toward sexual equivocation.

This equivocation should come as no surprise. The most visible champions of Roman Catholic orthodoxy have always been portrayed as strongly and capably masculine, while beneath their ermine robes there lingers the musky scent of homoerotic desire. Whether they be pope, bishop, theologian, or saint, their shrill clamors for sexual uprightness and doctrinal certitude go hand-in-hand, bespeaking their own ambivalence and confusion. But reality always shines through, and the cassock is sooner or later revealed as the drag out-fit that it truly is. It therefore makes perfect sense that the angelic guardian of the Church of Rome should be so sexually charged in his masculinity, but that he also carry a suggestion of same-sex ardor and desire, of gender ambivalence and erotic ambiguity. He is, after all, protecting the assets of men-loving men.

As with most archangels, Michael's wings are massive, and they are often shown as brightly multicolored. Angels are not humans, though they carry the human form, so the wings are the only outwardly visible sign of their difference, what sets them apart. Presumably, angels are also asexual beings. The wings, however, can symbolize the missing genitalia. In their sheer volume and size, and presumably in their power when they are deployed, Michael's wings are the mark of his virility and masculinity. In many ways, his wings are the source of his potency and might, and the one thing that gives him effective dominance over the obscure forces of evil. The raised phallus — here iconographically transformed into the symbolism of the wings — therefore becomes the real seat of power. Paradoxically, and perhaps intentionally, it is also on public display, the one sure part of an angel's body that we can see and that immediately captures our attention. Michael's strikingly beautiful wings, far from being the sign of his heavenly ethereality, are in fact the manifestation of his masculine identity.

Interestingly enough, the only truly masculine character among the angels is Michael's archrival, Lucifer himself (the name means "bearer of light"). Lucifer is nothing if not manly. In our imagination, we would never really think of associating the image of the devil with anything but extreme and unparalleled virility. In popular visual lore, particularly that associated with ancient witchcraft and satanic worship, Lucifer is physically huge, with a hypermuscular body. Images also depict him as particularly well-endowed. Testimonials of suspected witches during the European witch craze refer to the devil's penis as large and icy cold, and sexual intercourse with him as a painful experience. There is no doubt that the source of Lucifer's symbolic power is the phallus, as it is, in a more limited way, with the other archangels. Compared with the image of Michael in the iconography, however, Lucifer is a far more highly charged erotic figure. His body, his bearing, and his popular association with sexual excess and degeneracy confirm this. This certainly taps into, and is reflective of, Catholicism's body-negative ethos and its theological and cultural sublimation of "dangerous" sexual energy. But were it not for the association of Lucifer with evil — and with absolute evil at that — his stature and appeal as a homoerotic religious figure would not really be in doubt. It is interesting to note that legend has it that Lucifer was the favorite of God, the most beautiful of all the angels. In his arrogance, he defied his creator by refusing to serve him, and became an outcast because of it. But Lucifer has certainly maintained his appeal and his fascination for humans, more so than Michael, who stands as a bit of a second fiddle to the charisma and power displayed by his enemy. As is so often the case in human experience, evil is the more enthralling realm. I've often asked myself, in a silly theological way, how God may have felt about losing his favorite, and if he really didn't consider Michael a bit of a vacuous upstart.

A close look at the imagery of sexual appetite in gay erotica reveals how often desire is associated with darkness and the forces of imagined evil. Whether it be the fantasized gang rape scene or the character of the leather-hooded sadist, the strangely ambivalent sexual appeal of what most frightens us constitutes a staple of our imaginary erotic lives. In the extreme, we construct for ourselves stories of drastic sexual need and prowess, and we people them with larger-than-life sexually ravenous men. These men sometimes act as our fathers, brothers, or cousins. At other times, they incarnate far grander types of masculine, almost fantastic attraction. Among these, one occasionally catches a glimpse of a horned beast or god, a creature voracious and all-demanding in his brutish appetites. We so often become this god's willing sacrifice. We may stand with Michael, but we invariably lust for Lucifer. We may choose light over darkness and good over sin, yet we hanker for the vice that brings its own reward.

Michael and Lucifer represent opposite cultural poles. The former is all radiance, virtue, and orthodoxy. The latter, on the other hand, denotes sheer chaos, infamy, and subversion. In a sense, they need each other, just as religious culture (or perhaps culture generally) seems to require the contested binary poles of good and evil. In a certain Catholic culture of the 1950s, this duality was embodied in the image of Saint Michael the Archangel as the shining stalwart of righteousness standing strong against godless and Satanic communism. How much this imagery of Michael as fighter and religious "good guy" may have influenced me or other young gay boys growing up in that era is hard to determine. As Catholics, we already stood at the margins of American culture. We had few tools or insights to help us make sense of this reality, and those we had were, by default, religious ones.[6] In this context, the image of Michael as defender of both Roman Catholicism and the American way of life may appear somewhat ironic, though it does make eminent sense as a cultural response to the experience of otherness.

American Catholicism was, at that time, a suspect creed. The assumption was that your first and primary loyalties were not to the government of the land, but rather to a foreign autocratic religious regime. This was undoubtedly a false and stereotypical reaction, however different we may have felt. Yet our difference clearly made us feel outside the mainstream, which is why we became suddenly so certain of ourselves when John Kennedy ran for the presidency. I recall we had a ritual as Catholic boys. We would take a campaign pin of Richard Nixon, his rival, fold it several ways, and each of us stamped and spat on it in turn. Though childish, this was a way for us to affirm our uniqueness in the face of what we perceived as a staunchly anti-Catholic campaign. No doubt in this battle, the shining breastplate and raised sword of Michael would have been our guide and champion.

Considering his preeminent role as general of the angelic forces in the battle against Lucifer, Michael is, above all, a military man. He does carry, however, a special sort of military bearing: that of a Roman soldier or gladiator. His attire attests to this, as do his weapons of defense. In the gay imagination forged during my generation and slightly earlier, the image of the Roman gladiator is an iconic one. How many of us don't still remember, with great affection and a tinge of desire, all those Saturday afternoon TV movies featuring grunting and slimly clad Roman soldiers; or the wonder and delight of staring, slightly open-mouthed, at Kirk Douglas in *Spartacus* or Charlton Heston in *Ben Hur*? How many of our young masturbatory fantasies were fed by these classical hunks in short skirts? Many, no doubt. Michael, though he may not have been able to compete on such exalted cinematographic terrain, projects some of the same carnal energy. There was a visual as well as an erotic continuity between the Catholic saint and the Hollywood idols. At one level, this was strictly image-driven; at a deeper one, however, there was a nascent unspeakable desire to be ravaged by Kirk and Charlton, almost as much as there was by the prince of angels with the big beautiful blue wings. The fact that they both wore that silly short skirt exposing those ravishing manly legs, or that shiny breastplate rippled like a muscular torso, certainly didn't hinder the leaps of the imagination. Michael, the angel-as-gladiator, is brother to the paradigmatic Roman military men of our erotic dreams.

At a deeper level, the image of a man in uniform, be he the prince of angels or some matinee idol, stirs gay fantasies of authority and possession. Military men, police officers, firefighters, airline pilots, to say nothing of the paradigmatic icon of the sailor in the gay imagination: all touch on our fascination with, and ambivalence toward, strong and dominant images of masculinity. They reflect our unconscious need for protection and acceptance, a craving rooted in the unsettling memories of our sissified boyhood. We play with these figures, making them fodder for our darkest and most sustained erotic dreams, and endowing them with superhuman sexual qualities, hoping that they will make us more manly and desirable like them.

The Roman Catholic cult of Michael the Archangel reflects a complementarity within the worldview of the church itself. On the one hand, it points to the church's tenacious preoccupation with institutional consuetude and strength of tradition, while, on the other, it is suggestive of a spirituality centered on the individual believer in perpetual struggle with the demonic forces at large in the world. Prior to his exalted standing as a symbolic bulwark against "atheistic" modernism and Communism in this century, the manly warrior-angel really came into his own during the Catholic Counter-Reformation, when his fighting spirit was intended to mark the church's aggressive stance toward Protestantism. The gladiator-archangel represented besieged Catholicism "at war" with the rapidly encroaching Protestant hordes. Protestantism, in this staunchly Catholic view of the world, was equated with all that was diabolical and evil, and Saint Michael the Archangel, just as he defeated Satan at the beginning of time, would lead the Catholic offensive against this doctrinal deviation. This was Roman Catholicism at its most triumphant and regressive, and Michael was its perfect totemic expression. Here was the faithful and charismatic leader of the angelic hosts come once again to do battle with the legions of darkness.

But Satan, whether in the form of Protestantism or some other more mundane temptation, was also out to conquer individual souls, and Michael had the job of assisting individuals to overcome the devil's wily ways. A fairly typical Catholic prayer to Saint Michael read as follows: "Saint Michael the Archangel, defend us in our struggles. Be our protector against the wickedness and ambushes of the devil. May God command him, we implore, and may you, Prince of the heavenly militia, by the power given to you, hurl into the fires of hell Satan and all the other evil spirits who roam the world seeking the loss of souls. Amen."[7] The world, in this prayer, is indeed a dangerous place, full of unseen and devious demonic traps. Not only must Michael defend the church as a whole; he must also come to the rescue of the lone and weak individual struggling with temptation. He is summoned as the defender of personal virtue and integrity, as the faithful companion helping one battle the forces of evil. The plea is made to banish the devil and his minions into the perpetual exile of hell. Michael therefore operates at two levels simultaneously. He is a collective icon of institutional and doctrinal purity, and an empowering model of personal fortitude. As he protects and defends the church against its enemies, real or imagined, so he stands guard over the souls of its individual faithful.

For gay men, angelic saints — saints with bodies that can only be imagined and fantasized about — are perhaps the most sympathetic and compelling of all heavenly icons. Other saints are much too full of "bones and blood," prepackaged figures who lived real lives, and whose religious representations cannot be perfectly molded to suit the erotic projections of the gay believer. Angels, on the other hand, stand as fresh canvases, the only visual requirement being the wings that define their nature as ethereal beings (though wing size can certainly give rise to some creative thinking!). All the more reason that the most exalted of all angelic creatures, Michael, should stir the gay erotic sensibility. He is chief and master, the one in command, the man who takes charge and who protects, the defender of the just and righteous cause, the object of desire both carnal and spiritual. He is also the one who, because of his unique military role, can be depicted as the brawny male in uniform and the source of unspoken youthful fantasies. Michael stands tall and strong, a revelatory sign of gay passion as potentiality.

It is certainly not unusual for gay men to fantasize about "the perfect man," that one individual who will bring sense and excitement to their lives. This perfect man reflects the combination of ideal personality traits and consummate physical attributes. He is the companion and mentor, just as he is the man who will stand by us in adversity and doubt — two existential conditions made especially difficult and dangerous by the simple fact of our marginal position in heteronormative culture. In the gay-centered pantheon of Catholic saints, Michael the Archangel stands, in many ways, as this perfect man: perfect because, in truth, he is only a projection of what, we think, defines physical and psychological sublimity. Yet it is precisely this ideal model that serves to inspire and motivate, and it is the image of Michael riding the heavens in glory that makes it possible for us to even begin to consider the viability of manly perfection. As an angelic being, Michael taps into our need for spiritual wholeness; as a handsome warrior, he summons us to stand by his side in a posture of silent adulation.

Portraying Michael as defender and champion is to represent him in the guise of virile masculinity. It is this notion of masculinity, that of the male figure as protector, that mirrors an unconscious desire we have as gay men, individually and collectively, to feel safe and secure, and that reveals the potential use of Michael the Archangel as a gay icon. As a community, we do not have very many religious archetypes. Some, such as our identification as a "tribe," make reference to a Judeo-Christian biblical discourse stressing our unique historical role; others, alluding to special individuals such as "two-spirited persons," are more culture-specific. There are personages, such as Oscar Wilde, Harvey Milk, or Matthew Shepard, who have even attained the uniquely sacred status of gay martyrs. All these, in some way, speak to an overwhelming need to give spiritual voice and vision to our common experience as gay men. From a catholic — that is, a universal — perspective, Michael, he who is "like God," the very image of hardy manly conviction, could exemplify strength and firmness in the face of another evil, that of homophobia. The sword-bearing, handsome archangel could be the one who comes valiantly to our rescue. He could be our "shield of righteousness" in our moments of adversity and rejection: Michael as both defender and comforter. Michael is also the favorite of the deity. In this role, he touches upon, and could reflect, our privileged role and place as gay men in the economy of salvation. In our identification with him, we also become favorites of the divinity, despite our status as sexual outcasts. A source of affirmation, this unique and positive position with respect to the sacred calls forth and makes possible a greater acceptance and celebration of our erotic difference. It points furthermore to a view of sexual difference as a moment of redemptive potentiality.

Michael also plays a part in another very interesting story of sexual difference and ambivalence, that of Joan of Arc. As a symbol of military prowess, his is one of the "voices" she apparently heard at the tender age of fourteen, encouraging her to "save France" (the others belonging to two legendary female saints who apparently never existed, Margaret of Antioch and Catherine of Alexandria).[8] How much the command and presence of the shining archangel may have been used as a religious source of justification for Joan's military mission is difficult to say, though it undoubtedly played a significant part. What is more interesting for our purposes is the fact that Michael was instrumental in clarifying the special life-calling of a saint who symbolizes, in several important ways, the epitome of the androgyne and the transgressor of gender normativity. In this sense, Michael the Archangel can represent, for gay men, the affirmation and validation of sexual variance, the angelic voice empowering all of us, on behalf of the supreme deity, with a measure of divine presence and worth in the world.

In today's vapid New Ageist culture, angels have become somewhat emasculated. They are seen as harmless guides and messengers, beings meant to protect and inspire us. They are nothing if not cute, ephemeral creatures whispering over our shoulders or intervening at critical moments in our lives to save us from harm or a bad business deal. This imagery says much more about our cultural anxieties than it does about the nature of the heavenly hosts themselves. What has happened to the manly angel, the one who personifies the will and wrath of the godhead, the strong, silent type, the agent of divine volition? He (for it has to be a "he") is no more. He has been replaced by the innocuous and colorless cherub, that chubby infant with undersized wings and no genitals in sight. Perhaps gay culture needs to reappropriate the angelic imagery, to give it character and soul, to endow it with manhood once again — in sum, to reclaim Michael, the prince of all the angels, as one of its own.

Interestingly enough, angels are not new to gay culture. One need only think, for example, of the dirty smirk and enticing erotic possibilities of Caravaggio's portrait of Cupid,[9] or of the winged creatures floating about in the images and words of any number of other gay artists. More recently, prize-winning gay playwright Tony Kushner, in his powerful play *Angels in America,* has very effectively used an entire hierarchy of angelic figures as a means of commenting on, and ultimately valuing, the cultural experience of AIDS. In the central moment of the play, the main character, who is HIV positive, has a titanic religious and erotic struggle with an extraordinarily massive angelic figure, meant to symbolize the power of alchemical insight and transformation.[10] Angels can, in fact, be very plastic cultural artifacts. Partly, this has to do with their identification with a state of human and divine liminality, of uncertain and fluid "in-betweenness." This, I would argue, makes them potent sexual effigies

37

with vastly unexplored transformative potential. As religious icons, they give voice to heavenly desires.

With Michael the Archangel, this liminality functions in terms of seemingly opposing polarities. On the one hand, he represents divine righteousness and power; on the other, he stands strong as a provider of comfort and protection. In his persona, he is aggressively military and masculine; in his imagery, he can be a beautiful androgyne. Angels are believed to represent attributes of the godhead. Such a godhead combining contradictory qualities is very attractive to gay men, accustomed as we are to treading a fine line between rival worlds. It makes Michael, the brightest among all angelic beings, one of our saints *par excellence*, the embodiment of our deepest and most compelling desires, be they erotic or spiritual.

The seminary was a place where I saw angels every day. They shared meals and playing fields with me. They stood in the shower with me, and dressed as I furtively averted my glance. They taught me to shave and tie a tie, and sometimes put their arm around my shoulder. They were boyish angels, smelling of unspent bodily fluids and postgame sweat. They obsessed me, and I only wish I had dared to touch their inviting, outspread wings.

As I lingered upon Michael's bronze statuesque countenance in my youth, I do remember that I would get an erection.

Blessed Michael the Archangel, favorite of the deity, carrier of light, stand by our side. Be our breastplate in times of doubt and uncertainty, when the world would rather we not exist. We know we have been blessed with a holy purpose. Cover us with your strong and gentle wings. Shelter us under your noble and manly cloak. Lead us in our battle against the fear and hatred of sexual difference. And may your angelic face smile upon us forever. Amen.

T W O

Sebastian and Tarcisius

MARTYRS, PARTICULARLY THOSE from the beginnings of Christianity, occupy a special place in the pantheon of saints. They
were, in fact, the first saints. Their tombs, on the outskirts of Roman
cities, were at the origin of what became known as the cult of the
saints.[11] The stories of their lives became paradigmatic for all subsequent writings and legends about saints. Very often, the more
gruesome and glorious the descriptions of their martyrdom, the
more inspiring their legends were thought to be. There was a colorful sadistic streak to much of this, as though religious piety were a
function of voyeurism. It has often been said that it was "the blood
of the martyrs," the earliest witnesses to the faith, that nurtured the
soil upon which the Christian church grew and spread throughout
the Roman world. There is undoubtedly much truth to this, as would
understandably be the case for the fallen heroes of any secular or religious revolution. These early martyrs, standing at the very heart
of the military and political colossus that was Rome, gave powerful
credence to the universalist claims of the emerging Christian faith by
negating defiantly the religious and political monopoly of the em-
pire's gods, including the emperor himself. It was divine vindication
by persecution.

In the self-conscious and defensive American Catholicism of the
1950s and 1960s, not only were we called to Christian sanctity; we
were also urgently summoned to martyrdom. I recall, during my
high school days, having seen a rather hysterical book decrying the

ravages of atheistic communism. Vivid parallels were drawn between the Christian martyrs and what those living under such a political regime had to endure. I remember one particularly compelling image of people being whipped by soldiers and set upon by ravenous dogs. The implication was that "the Commies" would do to us what Roman emperors did to the Christians if we allowed any subversion of the American way of life. Good was American; evil was Russian. It was simplistic but terribly effective propaganda. I knew nothing of Karl Marx and his perceptive and humane critique of injustice back then, but I sensed that all this hysteria was somehow a bit much.

The Christian martyrs, for me, had much more to do with hungry lions and mad emperors than with anything else. As stereotypical as this imagery might have been, it was, in fact, little more than a series of horror stories filling the wild imaginings of an impressionable Catholic boy. Horror, whether real or invented, both attracts and repels. Religious horror is particularly insidious in this regard. Under the veneer of pious and saintly devotion often lingers the sadistic streak of ruthless power being acted out. The dead, martyred victim emerges as the one saved, and more importantly in the case of Jesus himself, the one through whom such salvation is possible. The "monster" remains absolute in his claims upon the martyr and upon our imaginations, just as Nero stands secure yet enthralling in his legend as a bloodthirsty tyrant.

The iconography of martyrdom had a great deal to do with my response. I once visited a wax museum that showed a series of scenes of early Christian martyrs in a coliseum encircled by apparently ravenous lions and tigers, while others were hiding in the catacombs. The effect was eerie, even though the display was a bit tattered and dusty around the edges. I tried to imagine what it might be like to be in their position, and I didn't care for the feeling. It made me feel afraid and vulnerable, not at all confident in my faltering abilities to imitate them to the death. Years later, on two separate occasions,

I visited some of the original catacombs on the outskirts of Rome. My response was very different. These were times of spiritual recollection for me. I also recall, as an altar boy, being brought on a day-trip to a chapel in a small Quebec village which claimed to have the largest collection of early Christian relics in the world. It was overwhelming and slightly tacky. Every square inch of wall space had some glassed-in piece of bone affixed to it. We played a game, trying to figure out which martyred saint fit with which bone. The anxieties of our Catholic youth had much more to do with the weird and anonymous bones of dead people than it did with the heavenly aspirations of long-forgotten martyrs.

What they were said to have done to some female martyrs was truly hideous, having to do, no doubt, with the usual projections of thwarted male sexual craving: the cutting of breasts and gouging of eyes, the spikes in the flesh, and the raw assaults upon puerile virginity. Male martyrs, by comparison, were assured of somewhat more decent deaths by such "manly" instruments as arrows, knives, stones, wild beasts, and fire. Yet invariably, they were bare-chested in their pictures and often wore only a loincloth, as a shining, androgynous angel hovered above them with the martyr's palm. The ways in which Catholics were taught to envision the deaths of their martyrs had as much to do with sexual role-making and gender normativity, including homoerotic projections, as it did with hagiographic musings or just plain theology. Among the male martyrs, there were some given as models or patrons for different masculine stations in life, whether one was a military man or nothing but a simple altar boy. Such was the case for both Sebastian and Tarcisius. Martyrs can also be, and very much are, a reflection of social structure and class, just as they display subtle cultural readings of sexuality and gender.

The suffering and death of the martyr is what brings them glory and, by extension, what brings us, as believers, the promise and hope of an equally sublime afterlife. What is particularly striking

41

about depictions of martyrdom, however, is the almost obligatory and strangely attractive equation of pain and ecstasy, of agony and beatitude. Much of this has to do with a uniquely Christian take on suffering as a redemptive fact of life, particularly if it is accepted with open arms. An equally significant variable is found in the Christian understanding of the erotic life as something which, even though it remains highly suspect, opens up a certain measure of spiritual freedom. From our postmodern stance, the torturous throes of martyred bodies can appear erotic in the extreme, as indeed they were always meant to be. From these ambiguous images, desire is born, be it desire for spiritual union or the more problematic desire for sexual coupling.

Few Christian saints have exerted such pervasive influence in the realm of cultural production as Saint Sebastian. In the history of art, even to this very day, his image is encountered quite regularly. His story has inspired drama, music, film, and literature, both pious and secular, and the paintings of him are literally legion. His iconography is immediately recognizable: a semiclad youth, well proportioned, tied to a tree or standing with his arms bound above his head, pierced by arrows and gazing heavenward. It is the arrows that give him away, for legend has it that this was how they attempted to kill him. If one did not know the story, one could not tell that Sebastian, in his semi-naked state, was, in fact, a member of the Roman military elite. His legend therefore symbolizes the historic encounter between Roman paganism and sectarian Christianity, and tells how the latter effectively subverted the former from the inside. Sebastian was, in his origins, an engaging figure of cultural and religious controversy, and he remains so.[12]

In his classic study of gay male visual imagery in photography and film, *Hard to Imagine*, cinema scholar Thomas Waugh, writing about the decades following the Second World War, states:

The martyr, however, not the angel, is perhaps the most char-
acteristic mythic carryover from the Glamour Generation.
Photographers of the fifties such as Tobias and Lynes offered
more than their share of crucifixions, and Pasolini hammered
in more nails on every set. But Saint Sebastian towered above all,
transformed by pre-Stonewall artists from a minor saint of the
thirties into a profoundly rooted bellwether of fifties and sixties
erotic sensibilities. The images of the martyr — or in sexual sub-
cultural terms, the masochist — reverberate through the work
of this entire generation, inextricably fusing eroticism with the
representation of pain. After all, "passion" really means suffering, etymologically speaking, as theorists of the melodrama,
that other great genre of the fifties, keep reminding us. Influenced by Cocteau, artists such as Genet, Anger, Lynes, Tobias,
and Jutra all articulated intensely desirous erotic images of the
passive receiver of sexualized violence or power play.[13]

Waugh touches upon one of the more significant, yet too often
misunderstood, aspects of Saint Sebastian's iconography: that of his
compelling and recurring stature as a homoerotic ideal. It is Sebastian's physicality, above all, that captures one's attention. Here
is the male body at its most beautiful and erotic ravaged by arrows — unambiguous symbols of phallic power and dominance —
but still translucent and desirable in its grace and elegance. Here
are stark death and sadism, but ennobled to the point of sexual
hunger. Here is the martyred military saint who feeds (and affirms)
our fantasies about swarthy Roman legionnaires. Here is male desire
in its simplest and most eloquent manifestation, at once victim-
ized and glorified. The image of Saint Sebastian carries a complex
symbolism having to do with the hunger of men for men and its
necessary corollary of power and pain. Sebastian is a paradigmatic
queer, which is why one of the most famous Renaissance portraits

of him was painted by Sodoma, and why he can also be represented as a sailor, that other great homosexual icon, by twentieth-century French painter Alfred Courmes,[14] or by the more contemporary kitsch artists-photographers Pierre et Gilles. Perhaps the most significant literary reference to Sebastian is Yukio Mishima's *Confessions of a Mask*, which undoubtedly says more about the Japanese author's own tortured homosexuality than it does about the place of Sebastian in the literature of the East. Mishima's passages where he uses the image of the pierced saint as a source of nascent erotic desire are beautifully arousing.[15]

The actual legend of Sebastian is at once reflective of the essence of Christian martyrdom, yet quite fantastic in its originality. The iconography that has sprung up around it is equally ambiguous. Martyred under the co-emperor Diocletian (reigned 284–305), some stories refer to him as the emperor's favorite, a sort of sexual plaything. This hints at the question of physical beauty, though its historical accuracy is far from certain. Already, however, there is a homoerotic subtext in the construction of the legend. It is claimed that he resisted Diocletian's advances, thereby courting death. The far more common version — certainly more normative in terms of its theological and sexual template — states that he used his privileged position to convert upper-class Roman citizens, especially fellow military officers, and also to comfort Christians facing death. Regardless, he was condemned to death by being shot with arrows. The story goes that he survived and was nursed back to health by another saint, Irene. He once again confronted the Roman emperor for his paganism, and this time was martyred in a far more prosaic fashion by clubbing. His body was thrown in the open sewer of Rome. He was "twice-killed." This gives him very special curative and restorative powers in the popular religious imagination. After Saints Peter and Paul, he is the third patron of the Eternal City, thus placing him at the very center of Catholic religious geography.[16]

Popular devotion to Saint Sebastian became widespread in Europe because of successive waves of the plague. In fact, he was the saint prayed to as a defense against it. Two reasons can explain this: the fact that he was able to survive his first martyrdom, and therefore was seen as a source of healing; and perhaps more significantly, because the symbolism of arrows was linked to the widespread imagery of the plague "piercing" individuals as a punishment from God. The phallic undertone — the sexual ravaging by the hypermasculinized deity — cannot be underestimated here. The twin concepts of *eros* and *thanatos* (sex and death) have always stood in harmony, spurring artistic production as well as the most obtuse forms of spiritual and erotic ecstasy. Equally important, they have fixed the contours of the religious imagination, which is why Sebastian, in his flirtatious half-naked pose transfixed by the instruments of phallic death, resonates so powerfully in Christian hagiography, and why he stands so proudly at the center of gay culture. Sebastian is an even more necessary saint for gay men today. The time of AIDS is still upon us, and this saint, in his therapeutic and healing powers, becomes a patron, the one who would protect us from "the gay plague," so named by those who reject us with disdain and spite. Perhaps his religious potency could become our political force, and his prophylactic energy our haven of salvation.

The male body is certainly not something easily handled by religion. In its wild unpredictability and its phallic energy, it is a body most often ignored. As opposed to the female body, which is a source of intense wonder and sadistic control because of religion's oppressive heteronormativity, male physicality remains deeply suspect despite its all too apparent theological and ritual visibility. In the Christian tradition, the omnipresent image of the crucified god-man wearing only a loincloth is powerfully negated by the antigenital theology that surrounds his person. This portrait stands in vivid opposition to that of his mother, Mary, whose very identity is founded on her sexual omnipotence, even though it is a sublimated and virginal one. There are really only two other Christian saints whose sexuality defines their attributes so intimately: Mary Magdalene, who was said to be a whore and can therefore be depicted as nothing but naked flesh and flowing hair, and Sebastian, who was perceived as queer and can be represented beautifully bare-chested while being sodomized passively and ecstatically by arrows. The other important aspect of Sebastian portraiture is the ethereal beauty of the face. He is shown as handsome and young, at times slightly androgynous. Once again, as in the case of Saint Michael the Archangel, there is a clear and persistent ambivalence with respect to what constitutes masculinity, and how it can be represented both theologically and iconographically.

The wonder of the Saint Sebastian story is its elasticity, the fact that it has such a powerfully homoerotic subtext which, while so often negated, still manages to titillate. This subtext — especially in the eye of the informed, queer beholder — transforms the religious into a source of masculine desire. One can certainly pose two distinct gazes upon the story. The first is the typically hagiographic one of a confrontation between paganism and Christianity, with the defiant martyr being subjected to hideous torture and death while eagerly awaiting his heavenly reward. The second can give rise to all sorts of intriguing possibilities. What if Sebastian was, in fact, the emperor's favorite because of his physical beauty? Presumably, this means that he was no longer a virgin, and that he had already allowed himself to be seduced, physically and emotionally, by the allure of paganism. Was his death caused by his conversion to Christianity, or rather because he refused, for whatever obscure moral reason, no longer to give in to sexual demands of a particularly exciting sort? Was the martyrdom decreed by a jealous lover who chose death by arrows as a symbolic way of reaffirming and avenging his sexual conquest?

The very posing of these questions makes possible a queer Sebastian. It is not so much the official hagiographic discursive framework as the subtly hinted-at potentiality that actualizes the legend. If Sebastian were the lover of the emperor, and even if he were a Christian, then his martyrdom assumes a wholly different dimension. It is no longer exclusively a matter of sectarian Christianity confronting pagan arrogance, but rather of a struggle between two men desiring and possessing each other, to the ultimate destruction of one of them. In the end, it becomes a paradigmatic story about the hidden homoerotic and homophobic underpinnings of power and the destruction they can blindly wreak. The transpierced saint emerges not as a virtuous and straight Christian icon, but ultimately as a vulnerable and vindicated queer one. Queering Sebastian, though the artistic and hagiographic traditions may allow it, still entails a process of appropriation.

A few years ago, on the occasion of the Catholic jubilee, I visited the catacombs of Saint Sebastian on the outskirts of Rome, off the Appian Way. This is reputed to be the place where he was buried, and a major church stands on the site. Apart from the actual site of his tomb, surrounded by graffiti in honor of Saints Peter and Paul, whose remains were believed to have rested here temporarily, the highlight is the chapel dedicated to him containing a beautiful white marble statue of a Sebastian reclining in death from a drawing by the great sculptor Bernini. It is a strikingly attractive piece of religious art, at once ambivalent and arousing. A young, handsome male figure, half-naked and perfectly proportioned, lies on his side, with one hand covering his chest. Longish, curly hair surrounds a head slightly elevated, reclining on the breastplate and helmet of a Roman military officer. The almost naked body is covered sensuously by a rippling piece of cloth, leaving his sinewy legs and chest exposed, while three golden arrows protrude almost lovingly from his chest, biceps, and thigh. The saint looks as though he were asleep, or just napping after a bout of lovemaking. I was mesmerized. Here I was, standing at the site of Saint Sebastian's burial, totally engrossed by the beautiful yet saintly body represented by the statue. I prayed and lit a candle, kneeling in silent and holy adoration before this translucent image of masculine beauty.

My own engagement with the figure of Saint Sebastian arises from the sheer visual pleasure of contemplating a handsome male wearing only a loincloth. Mine is decidedly a fetishistic gaze. If he were a contemporary model strutting Calvin Klein underwear in some ad, the image would be equally arousing. Completely naked men do not engage me as powerfully, though they certainly can be beautiful. Men in underwear bespeak the dormitories and locker rooms of my boarding school days, my father sitting at home, my boyfriend in bed. They give voice to nostalgia and innocence. There is nothing more masculine or alluring than underwear, nothing more private or hinting at the secret vices of forbidden pleasure.

Sebastian remains my icon. I have pursued his image in several of the world's great museums, my eyes ever alert at a distance to the raised arms and pierced torso. I go on pilgrimage, seeking, like a talisman, the comforting embrace of his ecstatic, saintly gaze. I examine carefully the pose of the body and the position of the instruments of death, those arrows so firm yet flirtatious in their murderous intentions. I can recognize the different styles of Sebastian iconography, and the periods in which they were painted. I peer at the loincloths, hoping to detect in each the timid outline of the holy tumescent member. My eyes reach out to enfold and embrace the martyr, to heal his sacred wounds, to place his dying head on my comforting shoulder. Desire speaks. If only he were mine. If only he were my saint, my man, my lover.

A considerably less well-known saint, though an important one in the pantheon of young Catholic martyrs, is Tarcisius. As a seminarian, I recall the wooden statue of him that stood near our dining room. It always had a light shining on it. The statue was of a boy our age dressed in the short Roman toga, with a shawl around his shoulders and his hands clasped underneath. This was an obvious reference to his death. He was carrying the Eucharist to sick Christians in Rome when he was set upon by a mob demanding to see what was hidden so carefully beneath his cloak. Legend has it that rather than give up the consecrated host to be desecrated, he accepted martyrdom.

The statue was meant to inspire us in our young vocations. The seminary was run by a religious order dedicated to the cult of the Eucharist, and the example of Saint Tarcisius suggested that we should be equally prepared to die defending the body and blood of Christ, or at least that we should be as pious and single-minded in our devotion to them. I always found this young Roman martyr a bit of a puzzle. His story is virtually unknown, so little can be said about him. How he may have lived, if he was a recent convert, or even if he really did die the way it is claimed — all these questions remained unanswered, almost as though it was up to a boy's wild imaginings to fill in the gaps. The model of Saint Tarcisius was also suggestive of the special place which boys occupied in the Catholic cultic hierarchy, that of the altar boy.

Prior to the reforms of Vatican II, only boys were allowed to serve at the altar. This was a form of privilege, a copy of the men-only regulations governing the ordained clergy. Altar boys were really miniature priests in drag. When I was twelve, I would wake up at 5:00 on snowbound winter mornings to serve the 6:00 a.m. mass at my parish church. It was quite the thrill for me to walk around in a cassock and surplice, pretending to be a priest. In a way, I was preparing for my days in the novitiate when I was obliged to wear the cassock, even though, by then, I had rejected it in a spirit of liberal defiance. As an altar boy, I learned all my responses to the prayers in Latin by rote, and every gesture for serving the celebrant was meticulously choreographed. We were an elite in the parish. I felt I was participating as a significant player in what it truly meant to be a Catholic, with all the campy ritualistic performance that this implied.

Altar boys, or minions like Tarcisius serving the central Catholic ritual that is the mass, reflect the subtle homoerotic ambivalence of institutionalized Catholicism. Altar boys are servants of celibate men, malleable vessels for the transmission of sexualized men-only values. The mass, at that time, was an intensely charged *mise-en-scène*, an erotic stage of masculine desire and possibility. The distance from the sacristy to the altar, with all that the former implied by way of whispered and secretive gropes, was not that great; the latter simply extended and ritualized the ever-present erotic charge of the former. Of course, I was not conscious of any of this while I was playing at the altar. My heart was intent solely on serving the priest to the best of my ability. My thoughts were turned to the mysteries of the transubstantiation — to the apparent wonder of the god-man becoming bread, and to my desire to eat him and make him one with my body. But I was grateful for the presence of these older men around me, and I shivered with delight and childish expectation when they sheltered me in their fatherly arms. Now, many years later, I am reminded of the sweet and sorrowful story entitled "The Priest and the Acolyte," long attributed to Oscar Wilde, but written by John Francis Bloxam.[17] It tells the moving tale of a priest/minister and a very young altar boy who discover love together, though death invariably comes between them. Though my times as a server at mass were certainly not as melodramatic, nor as erotically charged, they still fired my imagination as sites for the acting out of my priestly desires and potential vocation. I was serving celibate men in order to be like them some day, carriers and servants of an overwhelmingly wondrous and mysterious power.

What Tarcisius makes possible by way of a model of gay sanctity is his proximity to the cult of masculine power and privilege. That is what we were being taught by his statuesque representation in the seminary. We were encouraged to be boys serving men under the guise and duty of religious ritual. We were called to an active engagement and identification with the paternal figures of our childhood and adolescence. We were the receptacles of the spectacle of male desire, and Tarcisius's utter passivity in the face of his own extinction was a model of life held out to us. We too, like him, should be willing to lay down our lives for the raw privilege of ingesting the body and blood of the male of males. We too, like a scout or a military cadet, should always stand prepared to serve and, by implication, "to service." Saint Tarcisius, the effeminate and uncertain boy-martyr, patron of first communicants and other liminal religious categories, silent and willing victim of rapacious pagan violence, was, for us and for our seminary mentors, a conduit of sublimated pedophilic delight and promise. He was the servant of servants, the boy not quite sure of where he stood.

There is another sense in which the figure of Saint Tarcisius evokes the sweet memories of queer Catholic youth. His death was the result of an encounter with a roaming gang of nameless Romans. We can let our imaginations run wild. Was he, in fact, beaten up by Roman teenagers intent not so much on desecrating the host, as on jeering the boy for his oddness and difference? Was this really an attempt at gang rape gone amiss? Did the young martyr die because he was protecting the unplucked blossom of his virginal anus? Has the legend been transformed from the image of one defending his corporeal integrity to that of the young saint safeguarding the new Christian god's sacred body and blood? The metamorphosis does not appear so strange after all. Many of us undoubtedly remember encounters with the bullies of the schoolyard in our youth. Though perhaps not as violent as what happened to Saint Tarcisius, we knew we were being picked on because our secret desires were dangerous. The bullies certainly knew it, which is why they wanted us so desperately and why they had to erase this knowledge with the bloody blows of their clenched fists. To allow, for one passing moment, the possibility of same-sex desire to emerge was to undermine a fragile masculine identity.

Martyrdom requires a victim and an executioner. Its discourse is that of power and altruism in synchronic, almost fluid exchange. When the symbol of the martyr is charged with latent homoerotic potential, as is the case with both Saint Sebastian and Saint Tarcisius, this power is at once political and sexual, and the altruism becomes vividly, powerfully paradigmatic. Martyrdom is an exemplary tool for spiritual transformation. Its potency is its very vulnerability, a vulnerability that exhorts and engenders change. For gay men, the queer martyr is, in sum, the queer man divinized, the faggot forever beaten and crushed, yet who thereby attains a state of immortal release and perfection. The queer martyr is ultimately a call to arms, an angry cry against a deadening, homophobic culture.

Perhaps Sebastian and Tarcisius really had known each other. Perhaps they were boyfriends once upon a time.

Blessed Saints Sebastian and Tarcisius and you other martyrs of the early church, pray for us. You who challenged and resisted the claims of mundane human power, stand by us. Our eyes are fixed on your beauty. Give us courage and fortitude. Enfold us in your nakedness. Soak us in your redemptive blood. As we stand before the cruel Caesars of this era, may we turn to you for strength and eloquence. And may your deeds be part of the stories of our lives. Amen.

THREE

John the Baptist

W HEN I THINK OF Saint John the Baptist, second cousin of Jesus, a number of images cross my mind, as though he were some sort of holy chameleon. The earliest and perhaps most meaningful, because it is tied into my own cultural heritage, is that of the aloof yet charmingly depicted political icon who reigns as patron saint of French Canada. Another conjures up the wild and intensely desirable prophet portrayed in the Richard Strauss and Oscar Wilde opera, *Salomé:* a man whose religious zeal is the source of his sexual power. And the third, an acute reflection of my homoerotic sensibility, centers on the imagery of the brooding adolescent Baptist painted several times over by Caravaggio, an artist who struggled with his own wild and unpredictable nature. There is also, of course, the more traditional iconography of John the Baptist as the hairy, austere, half-crazed messenger and prophet of water who came to announce the arrival of the Messiah in the person of Jesus, and whose urgent call to repentance was total and radical. This is the Baptist of biblical theology and church orthodoxy, a figure whose centrality in the Christian story of salvation guarantees his peculiar brand of fame. There are almost as many Baptists as there are ways of depicting sainthood, or, at least, of envisioning masculinity.

This polyvalence only serves to underscore the importance of John the Baptist in Christian hagiography, and of his uniquely privileged position in the large pantheon of Catholic saints. Here we have a direct relative of Jesus, someone presumably of his approximate age, who finds himself at the very center of the messianic mission. Apart from the master icons of Mary and Jesus, the Baptist is the only other New Testament figure whose life is recalled by more than one official feast day in the Catholic liturgical calendar: that of his birth (June 24), that of his martyrdom (August 29), and the Feast of the Baptism of Jesus in the Jordan (early January). Despite all this, he has remained a somewhat elusive and forbidding figure, a saint whose true character is hidden, forced as he was to stand behind his better-known and towering cousin. I've always felt somewhat sorry for him, though his involuntary and alluring anonymity certainly makes all manner of supposition possible, which helps explain, in part, his dark erotic appeal. There hangs an aura of raw, sweaty manliness about John the Baptist. In large part, this stems from his persona and character as someone of high and uncompromising principles. In our culture, as in most others, maleness is equated with firmness of character and singularity of vision, almost as much as it is with size of biceps and strength of body.

In the acknowledgments to my 1990 doctoral thesis on the national celebrations of June 24 in Quebec, I wrote the following: "When I was significantly younger and my mother was still alive, I recall that, on June 24, our family would visit an aunt who lived close by, in order to watch *la parade de la Saint-Jean* (the Saint John the Baptist Day parade) from her front porch. Everyone would anxiously await the arrival of *'le p'tit saint Jean* (the little John the Baptist) on the last float. As nostalgic as one invariably is about the years of childhood, those moments remain precious for me."[18] As mentioned earlier, John the Baptist is the patron saint of Quebec; his June 24 feast day is a national holiday, much like July 4 is for Americans. Traditionally, there was (and still is) a large parade held on that day. In a more religious past, the last float was the one that carried the figure of the Baptist. Invariably, a prepubescent, curly haired boy, usually blond, portrayed the saint. He was accompanied by a lamb, symbol of Christ. This manner of representing the Baptist was consistent with aesthetic canons of the times, borrowing as it did from religious and artistic imagery of earlier centuries, which often painted a young John the Baptist frolicking with his equally young cousin under the watchful maternal gaze of Mary. The arrival of the child-saint's float was the long-awaited highlight of the parade. For me, however, it stood as the symbol of a strange ambivalence. How could I reconcile this young sexless creature with the virile Baptist of my imaginings: the savage, hairy, and vigorous man who cuts such a dashing and commanding figure in the biblical stories? Though these were the hidden sexual musings of a queer boy, desire was still at work. I knew instinctively that the child-saint, though he may have been my age, was not who I wanted. He was much too tame and insipid for me. I much preferred and coveted the body and hands of the mature, beguiling saint.

Erotic ambivalence is, in many ways, one of the essential though hidden qualities of sainthood. Because we have such a difficult time imagining (to say nothing of allowing) saints as possessing any overt sexual nature, we deny this aspect of their personalities by means of a variety of discursive and visual strategies. Certainly one of the more effective is to represent them as children. This has the dual advantage of reaffirming the primacy of sexual innocence, if not ignorance, as a condition of sanctity, as well as transforming the object of devotional piety — the saint himself or herself — into the more malleable and less challenging, and thus more easily accessible, image of the child. Puerility begets comfort and certainty; there is no need to be unduly concerned about dangerous adult sexual feelings. Such a strategy has been used countless times in the cases of both Jesus and John the Baptist (less so for the Virgin Mary), most obviously through art. In such instances, we are allowed — even encouraged — to embark on a religiously sanctioned, though sublimated, pederastic relationship with the holy. Religious images of childhood are, at heart, symbols and occasions of primeval vulnerability awaiting corruption. They challenge us to sin in the most treacherous and damnable, yet ultimately satisfying, ways possible, but to do so by means of a safe and controlled religious environment.

As a religious and cultural theme, the corruption of innocence recurs throughout the West. It provides sublime paradigms of divine intervention, such as the rapture of young mortals by Greek gods and goddesses, or it gives rise to religious panic of the most odious sort, such as the myths and stereotypes with respect to infant sacrifices by both Jews and Christians, to say nothing of such contemporary urban legends as the Satanic violations of children. One also needs to ask whether the current debate around priests and sexual abuse is not part of this pattern. Yet the image of innocence embodied in the child — particularly that of the sinless martyr and saint, the helpless though willing victim of corrupt worldly power — continues to fascinate and titillate. Whether it be cherubs or the crowned Infant of Prague, adoring the holy child is a privileged way of entering into a sublimated form of erotic play with him or her, and thereby with the holy. This holy is best found in the transgressive. In doing so, we corrupt the ultimately pure and godly, for there is no other viably human way of apprehending it. From a religious perspective of mimetic sacrifice, only in desecrating do we venerate; only in violating do we honor.

This is a sentiment that Caravaggio expertly and knowingly played upon in his glorious series of paintings of the adolescent Baptist. These works reveal and confirm a powerful homoerotic sensibility to the artist. In each (there are at least four in existence), the image of the Baptist is that of a young man reclining half-naked (totally naked, in the case of one), draped in cloth of white and crimson. He casually holds a staff in the form of a cross, symbol of his prophetic role. The face is brooding and pensive, dark to the point of mystery. The portrait of the naked Baptist is engagingly erotic. In it, the saint fixes his gaze on the viewer. We can see the faint, shadowy shape of the penis and part of his ass. He is leaning on one elbow, looking over his right shoulder. Above him stands a ram, which he holds amorously by the neck. Normally, the Baptist would be shown with a meek lamb, symbol of Christ, the Lamb of God. Here we have an explicit symbol of male phallic power. The Baptist is caressing it and offering it to us as a sort of sacred talisman, a sign of conspiratorial knowledge and an invitation to partake with him of the promise of gratified male desire.

As a gay man, this image excites and moves me in turn. My immediate response is to the sensuous beauty of the boy, to his open and engaging invitation for sex. It is a visceral response, fed by a combination of raw physical desire and religious eroticism. I enter the portrait with shy trepidation. There sits the saint naked. Hesitantly, I approach. I love the look of his peasant face and of his carnal smile. His body is slightly bulky, the way I prefer it. I touch him shyly and gently. He shifts slightly, revealing a firming response to my contact. I immediately kneel, not daring to venture further. The saint stands in front of me. I raise my gaze to the glory of his aroused body.

In the course of a recent visit to Rome, I once again contemplated the original of this painting in the Capitoline Museum. It was a marvel. As I stood before it, the figure of the Baptist pulsated to my unspoken desires. It is a wonderfully unorthodox painting. Normally, the precursor of Christ would never have been portrayed as a naked, lascivious adolescent. Perhaps it was the explicit wish of a clerical patron with slightly suspicious queer leanings which made it possible, and thankfully so. It is known that the model for the saint was one of the hustler boys whom Caravaggio often took as his lovers. This fact makes the painting doubly significant in its iconic status as a compelling affirmation and celebration of same-sex desire and love. I like that a sodomite cleric may have paid for it, and that the painter used his lover as the model. It reminds me powerfully that we are indeed everywhere, written beneath, and across, and over material culture, constantly subverting its empty heterosexist, normalizing claims.

As a child, however, I undoubtedly shared a large measure of affinity with the childish Baptist in the parade. I may even have been jealous, wanting to replace him so I could be equally loved and saluted by those countless spectators along the route. My response was more one of awe, as I recall. I suspect the differentiation between boy and saint in my young mind was not really fixed or clear-cut, hence my sense of religious deference to the saintly icon. Here, in fact, stood someone my age who *was* the patron saint, who embodied the values and aspirations of an entire national group. In my mind, and even though I really knew better, there was no other way of possibly imagining Saint John the Baptist than in this guise of a cherubic youngster. In some ways, it was a very empowering religious symbol for a child on the verge of entering the seminary, as I was at that time. My vocation to the priesthood and to the privilege and honors that it held in store for me merged with the image of the child-saint on the float and the reverence and homage he enjoyed. Though I could not be the Baptist of the parade, the hero of the day, I could still be, as a potential priest, the headliner and golden boy of tomorrow.

I liked the fact that the child was invariably blond. To this day, I have a particular weakness for blond men. Though I am not sure if there is a causal link, it does strike me as somewhat interesting that I have always retained this particular fetish. It is obvious that I was responding to a specific, though limited aesthetic standard. In our Western view, we associate blond with light and what is good, with superior beauty of both body and soul. Blond men appear more wholesome. It also tends to be a shade associated with youth. Though personal taste is entirely subjective, and its origins are hard to locate with any measure of precision, it emerges in a specific cultural context, subject to the symbolic codes and social vicissitudes of that culture. In my view of the world, a blond John the Baptist was in the same erotic league as a blond Robert Redford, which was an immense turn-on in itself. We know, of course, that the real Baptist would have been anything but blond. He was, after all, a Middle Eastern Jew, and he no doubt had a distinctly swarthy Semitic look, much like Jesus. But saints have this other quality, apart from their erotic ambivalence, of also being culturally equivocal. This plasticity ensures their continued relevance, both devotionally and across disputed cultural boundaries. My Baptist thus stood before me blond and hairless, a youthful, though distant companion for a pious French Canadian boy on the uncertain threshold of adolescence.

I write this text on June 23, the eve of John the Baptist's feast day and Quebec's national holiday. Much has come and gone since those afternoons on my aunt's front porch in the early 1960s watching the small-town parade pass by. For one, the parade has been radically transformed. It now takes place at night, and the figure of the Baptist is nowhere in sight. This says more about the radical secularization of Quebec society than it does about the perennial attraction of parades. For another, I am now a fifty-year-old gay man. My reflections about Saint John the Baptist, particularly as national symbol, are more nuanced, perhaps more universal in their implications. Certainly, they no longer link the precursor saint with the national identity, though this historical phenomenon and its transformations continue to interest me as a sociologist of religion. The gay pride parade has replaced the one of June 24. The identity and politics are no longer narrowly political, but cultural in the broadest sense of the term. It is from my being gay and out that my pride flows.

Then and now, however, it is the hairy, adult-sized Baptist who has continued to haunt my erotic fantasies, and he is most definitely not blond. He is, in fact, very much the dark, mature man: a paragon of princely masculinity. And he is quite sexy in his role, as mysteriously aloof and attractive as only a genuine prophet and object of desire can be. If I were to fall for someone now, he would have the look of the dark Palestinian beauty, the haunted, desperate hunger of the exiled god, the prophetic voice and face of Middle Eastern marginality.

The opera *Salomé* plays very persuasively and vigorously on the theme of the remarkably close affinities between erotic desire and prophecy, between the power of sexual attractiveness and the authority of individual conscience. The scene is the familiar biblical one of the martyrdom of Saint John the Baptist, brought about by Salomé's sensual dance and Herod's lustful fixation and inability to deny her wish for the Baptist's severed head on a platter. In Oscar Wilde's original play and subsequent libretto, the focus is on the overwhelming physical attraction that Salomé has for the imprisoned Baptist, and how his rejection of her advances seals his fate. As in much else of Wilde's work, "Each man kills the thing he loves."[19] Several of the scenes between Salomé and the Baptist are highly charged sexually. What Wilde has done in his creative spin on the usual story line is to highlight quite forcefully the powerful attractiveness of individual conscience and moral rectitude, an attractiveness that he couches in the sublime language of eroticism. This theme is not new. In literature — as in our own considerably more mundane lives — one encounters the strong, silent hero: the man who is a turn-on simply by virtue of his self-assurance and calculated absence from the common concerns of everyday existence. As we all know only too well, a cultivated distance can be an amazing source of sexual power over others.

Another appealing theme in Wilde's treatment of the Salomé-Baptist story has to do with how evil must invariably corrupt, and even destroy, what is good and pure, a sadly prophetic vision that Wilde must have applied with some bitterness to his own unfortunate circumstances. In the end, he forces us to examine — and, more importantly, to acknowledge — our erotic subservience to the ineffably pure and to the destructively masculine. The figure of John the Baptist is a stand-in for the unspoken and too often uncontrollable desires of our lives. For the opera is very much about desire: desire for the body and kisses of another; desire for the touch of the holy; desire for the forbidden and the unattainable; desire for the transgression of boundaries, whether they be familial, religious, or sexual. In this sense, Wilde was able to tap, scandalously and gloriously, into the real conflict at the center of this oft-repeated biblical tale, a universal and eternal conflict of human desire and divine grace.

I imagine and desire my Baptist much as Salomé did hers. I do crave to kiss his sensuous lips, as she did his. I so want to dance for him, turning my body into a source of pleasure and lust for him, as she did for her stepfather, Herod. I do need to smell his pungent body, the sweet elixir of masculine sweat and semen. I so crave to touch his coarse and oily skin, a tactile hymn to male beauty. I do want to spend myself on him, to tangle my fingers in his gnarled hair. I so need to seize his erect sex with my hand, caress it madly, staining myself with its generous effusion. I so crave his thick and dirty fingers in my mouth. I do want to be seized and ravished, baptized in blood, and water, and semen, and grace. I so want to stare into the face of a saint and cry my desire. I do need, and want, and crave, and covet, and desire the wild man of the desert, the prophet of my dreams, the lone messenger of the crazed gods of the Sinai, the gods of my destiny with whom I must ever wrestle.

The Baptist summons forth a need for pain and destruction. Much as Salomé destroyed him for his prophetic arrogance, so I want to ravage him as I love him, raze him as I claim him, wrap him as I possess him. I'm not sure why, however. He stands there, in front of me, a big, hairy man, more than life-size. What else can I do but love him in the most perverse way possible, as the dangerous, risky embodiment of dark masculinity? I sit here really not sure what more I could possibly write about him as a homoerotic icon. In many ways, he escapes my futile attempts at making sense of his place in our lives. It may be that I'm bored with him, as I probably would be with any other man so aloof and righteous. Why can't I simply seize him in all his apparent and contradictory greatness? I think of John the Baptist, and I immediately see this bulky slab of male flesh, an unapproachable figure who stands looking faraway, antipodal from the concerns of common mortals. It really is no small wonder that there never developed a popular devotional cult around him. How could it? This saint is simply too cold and virtuous. I am reminded of this person I once picked up in a bar: huge and immensely well-hung, but completely unable to utter two sensible words. After he had come, his sole concern and most pressing need was for food. He was an adult child; everything was instinctive and full of immediate cravings. Is this what the Baptist represents in some perverse sense: the boy-man who acts and responds only on the basis of his instincts, the savage whose natural desires both attract and repel us? Perhaps that is why it becomes so difficult, ultimately, to circumscribe him. He simply lies there, expecting to be pleasured and gratified by an adoring devotee. How altogether boring! But also, how deliciously enticing! If I were to "paganize" John the Baptist, I would transform him into an ever-horny satyr or the ever-erect god Priapus.[20] I think he would be the type to spend his days cavorting in forest groves with virginal young maidens and only slightly more willing, though well-experienced boys.

Reflecting on John the Baptist also makes me think of the Bears, that unique gay subculture which appeals to large-set, hairy men. They are a cuddly, harmless bunch. When I see their float in the gay pride parade, I find them strangely attractive. The most appealing thing about them seems to be their total self-acceptance, their complete lack of negative self-consciousness. They take pride in their girth and in their defiance of the empty canons of overly slim masculine beauty, as though these were unduly restrictive of genuine maleness. I imagine them in bed, rolling and frolicking in pounds of redundant flesh, like children playing with wet mud. It is a picture filled with sensual excess. They delight in hairy thighs, backs, and chests, in opposition to the hairless norms applied to gay men nowadays. I picture John the Baptist in much the same way: a fat (though he probably would not be, since he was a desert hermit) and hairy Bear. He is someone not afraid of standing outside the norm. If he were to make love to you (and it would be "to" not "with," since you would be expected to submit), it would be wet and he would be heavy, with sweat streaking down his face and dripping sweetly on yours. The Baptist is definitely a top. He would command that you call him "daddy." And you would willingly oblige, for you have long wanted to cry that name in a fit of unbridled passion. This is what the Baptist can bring forth: the breaking of boundaries and the transgression of limits, a liberation stemming from the negation of the interdict.

In history, excessive hair has long been associated with virility. Hairy chests and legs represent boundless, overpowering masculinity. Symbolically, there is something close to the beast about them. The Bears celebrate hair: hair that is wild, hair that is everywhere and anywhere, hair that glistens with sweat. Iconographically, John the Baptist is nothing if not hairy. His prophetic calling is legitimized by his hairy virility. His divine authority rests on his shaggy countenance, like a mad and crazy seer, like a deranged visionary. It is certainly a patriarchal, almost sexist way of seeing things, as though superabundant locks were signs of divine election. Hair is natural for a man, the sign and guarantor of both his masculinity and his adulthood, though, strangely enough, baldness is considered sexy. We all look forward to our first beard, because it is a sign of our manhood. Shaving becomes a coming-of-age ritual, something we resent having to do on a daily basis in later years, yet cling to out of a deep and desperate sense of male identity. Hair can signify sanctity, as well as its reverse. Beyond the merely customary, it stands for masculine prestige and power. It can be many things at once, different for men and women: sensuous, dangerous, sinful, vain, authoritative, and a recurring source of physical and emotional strength. The fact that the Baptist, as with his cousin Jesus, is so often associated with hairiness points to a dark side in the equation. The hairy Baptist is really the priapic Baptist, a satyr roaming the land and ravaging its willing inhabitants, a big Bear standing erect and proud, staring arrogantly down at you. He is the tall, hairy stranger encountered in the silent darkness of night, the one truly showing the way, the mighty precursor of our dreams.

As a Christian archetype, John the Baptist is the great initiator, the one paving the path to the truth. As a gay icon, he could officiate over our lives in much the same way. All of us, in some manner, have had to be initiated in our desires for other men, whether sexually or simply emotionally. All of us have had to step out of the closet, and someone has usually held the door open for us. Someone has pointed the way, has taught us how it should be done, has shown us how we can relate to, and care for, others like us. Someone stood there at the beginning. Someone taught us the truth about ourselves, as frightening and overwhelming as it was at first. And after that, nothing was ever the same about us. We underwent conversion. We knew where we stood and what it meant. We had been initiated into our truth, baptized with bodily fluids into our real family. The Baptist's call was also a call to conversion, and his sign was that of water, of renewal and the beginning of life. He stands guard over our comings out, the very first and all the ones we must subsequently face in the harsh course of our lives. He protects, and reaffirms our difference, for it is our only truth — he who came to speak for it, and to bear witness to it.

But it is not a meek and mild Baptist that I seek, the gentle precursor of an equally vapid and girlish god. It is the energy and power of males that I crave and summon forth. It is brooding and callous indifference and beauty that I yearn for, the sharp pain of desire unfilled and despised, the burn in the pit of the stomach, the loins bursting to give forth their seed in fits of raw ecstasy. For the gods and prophets of the Sinai are angry and vengeful, all-consuming in their hungry demands. They want lovers possessed by them and none other. They want you to crawl and beg, losing yourself in the ineffable beauty and lonely fear of their treacherous arms, filling you with their terrifying yet soothing grace. They baptize you in water and sperm and fire, and they brook no other god but them. For all else is vain idolatry, a mark of the unchosen and the cast away.

Of all the saints, it can be said that John the Baptist stands the closest to Christ. The affinities run deep. Apart from being second cousins, John was also the one chosen to announce the coming of the Messiah in the person of Jesus. He is the one Jesus turned to for baptism, thereby initiating his public ministry. He was the first real martyr, the first to shed his blood as witness, not to the Christian faith, but because of his stance against the public moral disorder of Herod. Jesus called him the greatest of the prophets, and it is said that he cried upon hearing of John's murder. John the Baptist is the original witness, the forerunner, the messenger, the one who has "come to pave the way." He therefore occupies a privileged niche in Catholic hagiography. He is a transitional figure, standing between the Old and New Testaments, and between one faith and another. As gay men, we are often forced to live disparate lives, at times simultaneously. We are often caught in the middle, between one type of private existence and another, more out and public one. We too are transitional figures, in-between people. Perhaps, in this place of liminality, we too have been chosen as harbingers of a new moral and sexual order.

On my desk stands a small wooden statue of John the Baptist which I bought in San Juan, Puerto Rico. It is a crude piece of work, attractive in a naive art sort of way. Clothed in a red tunic, his right arm points heavenward. In the other, he holds a staff in the form of a cross and a baptismal shell. He has huge coarse feet, long black hair, and an equally dark beard. Very classic, and very religious. It is the Baptist of my faith, but it is also the Baptist of my erotic desires.

I sometimes speak to him in the stillness of night. I ask him to show me how to submit to the wild flirtations of his handsome cousin.

Blessed John the Baptist, cousin of Jesus, wild and disturbing prophet, stand by our side. You who came to show the true path and to set our feet firmly on it, guide us in our uncertainties. We need your manly strength. As you baptized with the water of conversion and the promise of him who was to come after you, so we beseech you to open our eyes and our ears to the truth. Grant that we will never stray from it. In our doubts and fears as sexually marginalized persons, give us your beautiful shoulders to lean on and to strengthen us. Amen.

FOUR

Joseph

I'VE ALWAYS THOUGHT OF Saint Joseph as a bit of a wimp. How could a man allow himself to be suckered into believing that his virginal wife conceived a son without his intervention, and then decide to stay with her despite this? The Joseph of the Catholic Church has always been a rather exotic, faceless individual. He is the very model of simplicity and self-effacement, but also, in an amazingly paradoxical way, of purity and fatherhood. This Joseph is above all obedient. His mission was to guard and protect Jesus, and he did it by disappearing into the mists of history, so that his wife and son could take center stage. One does not readily associate this Joseph with virility or even paternity, though the latter is assuredly what he wanted to give the appearance of having accomplished. This Joseph is a paradox: a father without a real son he could claim as his own; a husband who, according to Catholic tradition, never had sex with his wife; a progenitor who did not really have a descendant. How else can one honestly try to understand poor old Joseph, if not as a bit of a pushover? Then again, do not many ordinary fathers remain faceless and nameless in their devotion to wife and children, thereby shrinking from view, almost as though they were never really and fully part of the biological equation?

Church teaching will tell you that humility is what Saint Joseph is really all about, that his greatness and sanctity come from his consciously having chosen to care selflessly and without fanfare for Jesus and Mary, that he was a man deeply committed to duty and an abiding sense of paternal responsibility. This orthodox image of Saint Joseph in Catholic theology and popular religiosity has to do with contested notions of fatherhood. The church's official teaching is quite straightforward. Fatherhood involves true sacrifice and self-abasement, not risky and slightly suspicious claims of masculine virility and sexual ardor. The erotic is sublimated. It should be channeled into care for the family and self-discipline, almost to the point of self-negation. Joseph's claim to fame, apart from having raised Jesus, rests on the fact that he was an asexual being, a perfect model of celibate fatherhood. His was a castrated paternity. Only a eunuch father, in fact, could pretend to sire a sexless man-god. This is the image that the church has traditionally put forward as the perfect model of what it meant to be a father. It is the thwarted though powerfully ideal image of the strong, silent, and humble type of father: strong to the point of sexual weakness; silent to the point of painful anonymity; humble to the point of an enduring oblivion.

The contrary discourse around fatherhood and paternity is one of sexual potency and true familial lineage. Here, the father, as head of the household, as paterfamilias, actively and deliberately claims the rights of progeniture. This view stands against the interests of the religious institution, which seeks rather to regulate family life, especially in its uncertain and messy gender and sexual dimensions. What better way to achieve this than by emasculating the father, its real and symbolic head? Not only does this apply to all human fathers; it pertains first and foremost to the man Joseph himself, stepfather of the unique son of God, and head of the holiest of all holy families. Joseph is, in fact, a sort of substitute father, the real father being none other than God the Father and Creator himself. It becomes fairly difficult to compete with such exalted company. Poor Joseph, always second fiddle! If anything, we should feel sorry for him. He did the best he could with what he was given. It was not his fault if his adopted son was also the seed of God.

Joseph

Saint Joseph's special role as eunuch-father and head of the paradigmatic family unit — himself, Mary, and Jesus — reflects not only
contested notions of fatherhood, but reaffirms also for the Catholic Church the centrality and fixedness of the heterosexual nuclear
family as a universal model. It is a delicate and fragile three-way relationship of dependence: submissive mother, absent father, oldest son
who is the unabashed pride of the adoring parents. It had to be a son.
An elder daughter would not have been worthy of such adulation.
Her gender would not permit pride of generation and descent. This
ideal family was the model for what all Catholic families should be
about: sexless, traditional, spiritual, and, above all, humbly focused
on the welfare of the eldest male child. The image of Joseph's fatherhood in classic Catholic iconography can only be understood in this
context. Here was a man whose only purpose was to lend biological
legitimacy to the man-god. There were undoubtedly other children
in this marriage. But since their parents, the better to be pure instruments of the divine will, were desexed, one never hears their voices.
Who needs to listen to them when the eldest son was God incarnate,
the voice of creation itself?

Montreal is the great world center for devotion to Saint Joseph.
On the crest of Mount Royal stands Saint Joseph's Oratory, a huge
pilgrimage complex first conceived by Blessed Alfred Bessette, better
known as Brother André, a healer and lay brother of the Congregation of the Holy Cross. The Oratory attracts visitors from around
the world. It is a religious site dedicated exclusively to the cult of
Joseph, with miracles apparently still being reported. It even pub-
lishes a pseudoacademic journal of Joseph Studies, or Josephology.
Visiting the Oratory is quite a surreal experience. The walls of one
of the first chapels are loaded with crutches and other parapherna-
lia for the disabled, silent witnesses to the intervention of the sacred
into otherwise prosaic lives. You can still buy the holy oil of Saint

Joseph, first peddled by Brother André as a tonic for various ailments. You can even catch a glimpse of Brother André's heart near his tomb, a bit of a standing joke in the city since the relic was stolen some years ago and apparently returned quite unexplainably. People maliciously claim that it is really a cow's heart. On sunny days, a small but fervent number of pilgrims mount the Oratory's countless central steps on their knees, expiating for some shameful sin or expressing gratitude to Saint Joseph for some inconsequential though apparently meaningful favor. The gift shop is loaded with tacky mementos of Catholic devotional life: glow-in-the-dark plastic rosaries and suspiciously effeminate plaster statues. Everywhere thrones the regal image of Joseph with the child Jesus in one arm and a white lily in the other. Paternity on the one hand; virginity on the other: the antierotic though masculine paradox at the very center of the Catholic family ethos, an ethos by and for sexless men.

Although the Oratory can be none other than an obviously Catholic pilgrimage site by virtue of its devotional practices, it manages to attract an amazingly eclectic and diverse selection of believers from a variety of religious traditions. It is not unusual to see Hindus or Buddhists, for example, respectfully touching the tomb of Brother André with their forehead, their hands folded in supplicant prayer. As with any space believed to contain sacred power, Saint Joseph's Oratory transcends the confines of denominational allegiance and theological orthodoxy. People come here because they believe that the place itself is holy, and that miraculous events can and do occur. Though it may well be Roman Catholic in both inspiration and outward expression, the Oratory significantly serves as a broader catalyst for an ecumenical encounter with diffused spiritual energy.

French Canadian Catholic spirituality adulated the figure of Saint Joseph. Every church and almost every household possessed a statue of him, the latter usually enthroned in the kitchen, and novenas and devotions to him were commonplace. March was known and cele-brated as "the month of Joseph" (as May was for Mary, and June for the Sacred Heart of Jesus). Saint Joseph was the first officially declared patron of New France, before Saint John the Baptist perma-nently usurped his position. Traditional Quebec society, until well into the early decades of the twentieth century, was rural, centered on agriculture and large families of upward of ten children. In this economic and ideological context, devotion to the Holy Family, and to Saint Joseph in particular, reaffirmed the centrality and stability of the family as the basic social institution and as a core cultural value. It was also indicative of a gender-based division of labor: the mother as educator and heart of the home life; the father as material provider and distant disciplinarian. Both my grandfathers were im-posing, proud men. I do recall, however, that they were also rather voiceless men, the strong, silent types of so much truth and lore. My own father has some of those same traits. From this unique perspec-tive of bread-winning fatherhood and mute masculinity, it was only natural that a voiceless Joseph should serve as their model and guide.

As a child, statues and images of Saint Joseph gave rise to feelings of security and gentleness in me. He always struck me as a kind man, the sort of individual one could trust almost implicitly. With the child Jesus in his arms, he gave off an aura of safety and protective love, the original sugar daddy. One felt quite certain that he would caress you chastely, whisper soft terms of endearment in your ear, hold you aloft in his big, rugged hands. Oh, such comfort! Joseph was also a carpenter, like my own father. He worked with his hands. He was a builder, a man's man. I undoubtedly transposed onto him some of my own incoherent yearnings for my father, many of which were certainly erotic in nature. As gay men, the figure of the father in our lives occupies a place of ambivalence. He is both refuge and challenge, authority and solace, nemesis and guardian. We see ourselves reflected in his confident masculinity, yet we know almost instinctively that it is not one we totally share. He defines us, yet, as all sons eventually do, we need to break with him. The father is the paradigmatic male of our world, the source and summation of our identity.

Psychoanalysis aside, there can be little doubt that the figure of the father beckons as a significantly ambivalent source of erotic attraction for us as gay men. Yet we fear saying and thinking this. The subject is taboo. The father as object of desire remains off-limits for us, something unspeakable, something forbidden and never to be transgressed. Yet, in many ways, this remains the source of the father's erotic power. Some months back, I was discussing this issue with a theologian colleague of mine. In the course of our lengthy conversation, we agreed that the reason I was blocked in my writing, and more precisely in this chapter (I had set this text aside for several months), was that I was unable and perhaps fearful of exploring what the image of the father meant to me in erotic terms, as a gay man. He was right. We agreed, however, that this was not only my problem. It was a fairly common experience for other gay men as well. The father is the first and most lasting image of masculinity in our lives. It makes sense that we should idealize him, and, in so doing, secretly desire him. But we remain shameful of this, because it fills us with a heady mixture of guilt and unspeakable longing. We spend our lives, some of us in vain, struggling with the delicate balance between filial love and incoherent urge.

Consider, however, the many erotic stories, on video and in print, that feature father-son situations, or the games we choose to play in the privacy of our bedrooms that revolve around this dynamic. The father is the first man with whom we fall in love. The voice of the father is the voice that first summons us to stand and walk. It is also the voice that teaches us the language of love and need, and, ever so subtly, the place of the erotic in the textures of our lives. He not only defines our understanding of masculinity; he also teaches us what power and desire are, and how to use them in the attainment of our ends. He is our protector and guide. He bathes us and caresses us, soothing away our childish hurts and tears. He is our initiator into the mysteries and rites of manhood, the totally other who is so much like us. As we struggle with our own sexual persona, his is the grown-up penis that we find so awesome. For gay men, our father-son games are games of wild longings and buried desires: spoken games for unspeakable acts. I learned to speak desire from my father. I copied the words he uttered and the sounds he made. I still do, alone or with others.

For some gay men, the image of the father can also imply homophobic rejection and intolerance, the intimate stranger in our lives who can snap us with a word of hate. How many of us growing up have had to live with the word "sissy" thrown at us from the angry, spiteful mouths of our fathers? Some boys are forced to break with the paternal figure from an early age, precisely because they reflect back to the father an unsettling and perilous image of himself, that of the latent or deeply closeted homosexual. Much homophobia, as is well known, stems from insecurity and the internalized fear of what the other tells us about ourselves. For gay boys or men who are abused or otherwise rejected by their father because of their sexual choices or identities, the challenge of paternal intimacy can become a prison, a never-ending source of angst and personal fear. This desire for closeness and parental approval becomes transformed, of necessity, into hate, though it is very much a saving one. It is the hate that tempers the steely resolve, the precursor of ultimate forgiveness.

For straight fathers and gay sons, the challenge of intimacy is that of a tenuously delicate balance between, on the one hand, unspoken though aching desire and, on the other, manly and confident companionship. Most of us somehow manage this awkward though necessary counterpoise throughout our lives, never really daring to confront or even imagine its true ramifications. Straight fathers and gay sons sadly remain strangers at heart. Gay sons can therefore spend a good part of their lives trying to seduce their fathers, not in any overtly sexual way, but through the devious devices of career and worldly accomplishment. We somehow still have to prove to them that we are real men, after all. So we become lawyers, accountants, or doctors; we write books that they will never choose to read; and we sometimes make or, somewhat more contemporaneously, adopt babies. We try to do what real men should do, and we try to be like them, men of whom we think our fathers would approve. This sweet game of wanting to please the single most important masculine figure in our lives, this game of lingering desire and sublimated longing, can carry us far. Yet it always brings us back full circle to the one whose presence towers over that of every other man: the figure of the eternal father.

Masculinity and fatherhood can of course be understood in terms of a sexual presence. Women's sexual energy is often spoken of and honored in reverential, quasi-religious terms; men's tends to be dismissed, sadly and perhaps too conveniently, as either patriarchal or pornographic. Yet the tradition of the sacredness of male sexual potency has a long and distinguished lineage, and is even present, surprisingly enough, in the supposedly asexual Christian heritage. Though Jesus may have been celibate, as some prefer to claim, there can be no doubt that his power was rooted in his intensely dynamic and confident masculinity. Though God the Father may not have a real body, he is still seen as progenitor and creator, and his seed of life assumes the form of a sacred bird that impregnates. Joseph is the one paternal figure who appears not to have a sexual persona, yet he must, of necessity, have had one. Consider, by way of example, his manly roles as provider and carpenter, head of household and educator to his divine son. I have a secret fantasy about poor Saint Joseph. I sometimes think that he really was quite handsome and sexy, a man with whom Mary madly fell in love, and who was as good a lover as he was a life partner. I think his son knew this, and that it was from him that he learned how to be a man, a truly exceptional one. I like to imagine a different Joseph, one not so faceless or anonymous, more confident and demanding in his presence as well as his needs: a Joseph with a phallus, as it were, much like those ancient Roman and Hindu gods whose sexual vigor holds the promise of their sacred power.

The persona and image of Saint Joseph are, quite naturally, all about fathering. For gay men, alienated as we generally tend to be from notions of progeny (something that is, thankfully, changing), fathering can sometimes be a rather exotic and far-fetched ideal. Yet, by looking closer and more deeply at our lives, we can discover that many of us "father" in quite unexpected and richly positive ways: from the mentoring of younger gay men to caring relations with our nieces and nephews, from the public witnessing of our sexuality to educating about safer sex practices. In my own life, I accomplish this most obviously through my teaching and my writing. If a single young gay man, taking one of my classes or reading something that I've written, can feel good and confident about his sexual choices and his identity, then I have been a father to him. Strangely yet beautifully enough, this is not much different from the experience of Joseph, who was father, model, and protector to a son not his own. The humble and selfless example of Saint Joseph reminds us quite eloquently of all that we already accomplish as surrogate fathers, and of how our lives as out and self-assured gay men can serve as much-needed paternal exemplars for those not yet able to walk or run of their own accord.

Mentoring is a skill and a gift urgently needed in contemporary gay circles. If mentioned at all, it is usually in the snickering tones associated with sexual initiation, in itself a necessary though rather limiting act. Mentoring goes well beyond such narrow confines. It touches upon issues of identity and shared history, of belonging and ritual, of responsibility and legacy. It teaches and encourages; supports and defends; motivates and inspires. It is how the old take care of and form the young; how they share the stories and myths of the tribe; how they ensure the continuity and survival of their communities. Identities are formed in such communities, and it is from them that rooted, fully human individuals emerge. While including a pedagogy of the erotic, gay mentoring must reach into the domain of symbols and rites: the lifeline of any vibrant, living group. It must not only teach technique; it must also inculcate meaning. What is the source and purpose of my difference? Were there others like me? How and why have we survived? What I am to do with this knowledge, for myself and those like me? Young queer boys and gay men ask themselves these questions, but seldom hear a positive response from their elders. As mentors, as "fathers," we all have a responsibility to answer, or at least create a time and a space for the questioning. I sense that Joseph did precisely that with his adopted son.

Some time ago, I visited the Hermitage Museum in Saint Petersburg. As the guide led us through the empty morning halls of the slightly decrepit imperial palace, before the mad onslaught of the uncouth, overpowering crowds, he stopped before one of the two Raphael paintings in the collection. I was wonder struck. Entitled "The Holy Family (Madonna with the Beardless Joseph)," it shows the traditional three-person composition of Mary, Joseph, and Baby Jesus. In itself, there is nothing unusual about this. The Madonna, young in appearance, holds a slightly rambunctious infant Jesus in her arms. The naked child is half-standing, half-sitting on his mother. Both are turned slightly to the right of the painting, staring at a strange figure off to the side. There, in the shadows, stands a much older Joseph, beardless and pock-marked, his head and eyes heavily turned downward, his hands leaning on a bulky walking stick.

One is first struck by the difference in age between the infant's parents. Joseph looks more like the grandfather of Jesus than his earthly father, and Mary has the chaste maidenly appearance of Joseph's daughter. Joseph is not looking lovingly at his wife and son. His eyes are cast down, in a posture of mixed deference and pious adoration. He seems to be suffering from some exotic skin infection, marked as he is by bumps and crevices on his drawn face. He does not have a beard, an artist's unusual departure from the canons of religious orthodoxy. In itself, this may have been a source of considerable dismay on the part of Raphael's artistic contemporaries. What amazed me above all was the look of fatigue and slight disdain on the face of Joseph. Here was a tired man, but also one on the verge of rebellion. Why, he seems to be asking himself, did I get stuck with this awful caretaker job? How did I ever manage to find myself with a virgin wife and a son with such a messiah complex? Why, oh why, did it have to be me? Existential questions, of course, that are asked by many of us every day, though perhaps not with the same exact words. But the sort of questions that one would certainly never associate with the humble and self-effacing Saint Joseph; questions of a slightly sacrilegious nature, in fact. I found it a stunning mark of Raphael's genius that he even dared to hint at these questions, and that he did not shy away from portraying the sheer exhaustion of a Joseph caught in the bizarre and unreal story that was his life. Here finally was a Joseph who was the very antithesis of what traditional church teaching said he was. Here, finally, was a human, grouchy, irreverent, and no longer silent Joseph, a Joseph much more of a man than a theological construct, a rebel Joseph.

From the uncertain mists of my youth, I also recall another image of Saint Joseph: that of a young and handsome man wedding his wife, Mary. It was a portrait that one occasionally found on holy cards and in the pages of older church catechisms, visual reminders of the belief that this very earthly marriage was also a heavenly arranged one: that Joseph and Mary, despite the unusual circumstances of her already being with child, enjoyed divine favor. I think about this image at this time of public debate about same-sex marriage, and the very strong condemnatory stance adopted by the Catholic Church on the issue.

It makes me mad to think about it, and to hear the hysterical and ridiculous claims of Canadian church prelates about incest becoming rampant if same-sex marriage is allowed by law, as though human civilization as we know it were signing its own death warrant. I am angry about all this "assumed" heterosexuality, this unfounded and silly belief that only opposite-sex love and commitment, despite all the negative statistics about the divorce rate, are normal and acceptable in the eyes of the Almighty, and that same-sex love is somehow inherently deviant and corrupted. It is at times like these that I want to tear up the image of the chaste marriage of Joseph and Mary, and to throw its tiny pieces into the smug faces of all the bishops and archbishops of the land. How dare you? How dare you stand against our rights as full citizens? How dare you call my love and my life choices decadent and unnatural? I know that Saint Joseph, himself a sexual outsider, would share my pain and anger.

In Saint Joseph's Oratory, next to the old chapel, there is a very hot and muggy room that is at the symbolic heart of the shrine. Dominated by a large statue of an open-handed Joseph, the hall-like room contains thousands of vigil candles that pilgrims and devotees have lit in honor of their saint. The air reminds one of a sauna. On the pillars are crutches and other *ex-votos*, testimonials to his miraculous interventions. Along the walls, at regular intervals, one finds large art deco plaques depicting the various titles which Joseph possesses: help of families, protector of the church, comforter of the sick, inspiration for a good death, and so forth. You can choose your shrine and light a votive candle in front of it, depending on the part or attribute of Saint Joseph from which you are requesting a favor. Near the exit door, the plaque is for Joseph, defender of virgins. Not many people kneel here, and there are fewer lit candles than at some of the other small shrines along the walls, a reflection no doubt of the oddity of virginity in our day and age. The religious iconography is interesting. Under Joseph's extended cloak, there are figures of nuns and young girls, and, quite unexpectedly, some of young men, with and without clerical collars. Virginity was a virtue almost always associated with young females in the Catholic popular imagination of the early twentieth century, though young males obviously needed the same protection from the saintly Joseph. Perhaps for males at that time the struggle was an even more formidable one, given their supposedly innate tendencies for sexually impure thoughts and misdeeds, and the restrictions imposed by the dominant Catholic culture. Regardless, this particular Saint Joseph defends them both, conscious as he is of the urgent need to cover their youthful and fragile sexual cravings with the protective cloak of his own holy chastity.

The young men and boys depicted in this scene are beautiful. Their angelic faces are turned upward in a look of beatitude, and their prayerful hands are extended modestly heavenward in gestures of sweet supplication. They have the blue-blazer-and-tie look of boarding school chums. Curiously, there are no older priests or religious in this pious assembly, only adolescent males. Presumably, older males either do not need the help, or they stand beyond redemption. In staring at this scene, you invariably ask yourself what it is that these young boys need to be defended from. It doesn't appear to be girls, nor can it be any of those more adult sexual tastes associated with the married state. Clearly, it has to be, as was known charmingly at a certain not-too-distant epoch, self-abuse: that terrible sin of the body so readily associated with teenage boys with raging hormones. Masturbation: the greatest of theological, cultural, and medical terrors, the burn-in-hell temptation of guilt-ridden Catholic boys, the act that makes hair grow on your palms, and that turns you senile before your time. This is the great seductive demon that the saintly Joseph can help good Catholic boys overcome.

As terrible as masturbation may have been to the obsessed Catholic mind, there was an even more unspeakable and dangerous temptation out there: special friendships, same-sex desire, homosexuality.

Surely, there were boys depicted on that plaque who had such feelings, or who may even have already submitted to them. Surely, Joseph would defend and protect them against such a damnable and perverse vice. Surely, their virginal bodies needed safekeeping from the devious, sickly designs of other, older boys, and perhaps even from those of their own teachers. Surely, the good and upright Saint Joseph, father of the young, innocent Jesus and chaste husband of the Virgin of virgins, would come to their rescue and give them fortitude in the struggle. I read the fear of homosexuality in this depiction of Saint Joseph as the defender of virginal boys. It is a sadly persistent Catholic fear born of sublimated homoerotic desire, of secretive clerical sexual craving channeled and disciplined into the paths of human sanctity. It is the same fear that condemns gay love. It is a fear born of recognition.

I turn to Saint Joseph as I do to my own biological father. I ask that the paternal hand be one of sweet, deliciously tender, and intoxicating caresses.

Blessed Joseph, humble and good man, father of the divine son, cover us with your paternal arms. As you served patiently and anonymously in guarding over your holy family, help us to care for others, especially those of us who find themselves alone and shut out from their own families. We beseech you, keep us in your fatherly gaze, and help guide us on the difficult path of our own masculine adulthood. You were a man of fortitude and discernment. Grant us these virtues. And as we reach out for the affection of our brothers, remind us always that love is gentle, wise, and selfless. Amen.

FIVE

Paul and Augustine

SOME SAINTS IMPOSE THEMSELVES by virtue of their charm and humanity. One need only think, for example, of Francis and Clare of Assisi or of Teresa of the Child Jesus. Others, however, dominate because of their exceptional character, though they may not be especially popular or likeable. There are many severe saints, individuals who have attained the heights of sanctity because of their imaginative or excessive mortification. In a category by themselves are what I call the intellectual or scholarly saints: founders and teachers, great theologians and writers. And then there is that rare breed of saints who, in some profound way, have literally revolutionized Christian belief, and whose pervasive influence is still felt. These are few and far between. It is in this category that one finds Saint Paul and Saint Augustine, men whose dominant personalities have fashioned the Catholic faith of today. They find themselves in this book, not because I especially like them, or they me, but rather because I have several bones to pick with them. They are inescapable, if only because they have been such a source of oppression for queer people. I have absorbed, consciously and unconsciously, more of the thinking and writings of these two theological bastions than I have any other religious thinkers. One simply cannot get away from them. And yet, I wish I could. We all do.

A big part of the problem stems from how these two men view the human body and, therefore, human sexuality. In the case of Paul, his righteous condemnations of same-sex desire (as well as his negative views of women) are certainly legendary, and are used time and again by all sorts of fanatics in their attacks on homosexuality, including those pronounced by the church herself down through the centuries. As for Augustine, his overwhelmingly influential philosophy of dualism continues to infect the outlook of the contemporary church on all things material, whether it be the isolated sex act or the very notion of pleasure itself. Paul is often said to be the true founder of Christianity. Augustine is its most modern and comprehensive thinker, Thomas Aquinas aside. Both have exerted incredible influence, and, some would say, unfortunately still do. Both are also superbly beautiful writers and theologians. So I stand torn and confused before both saints. On the one hand, I decry and abhor the harm they have done us. On the other, I am supremely grateful for their golden words. I stand much the same way in the church, as do, I would suspect, most Catholic queers.

The church of Paul and Augustine is most definitely the church of rejection and oppression for queer people. Though it be an exercise in rhetorical depression, one need only read the official Vatican teachings and pronouncements on homosexuality to grasp the full impact of their pernicious and hateful speech. Queer people are nonheterosexual and, therefore, not within the traditional theological paradigm of husband-wife as source of modeling for the church herself as Bride of Christ. Moreover, and no doubt far more problematic for institutional Catholicism, is our special relationship to nonprocreative erotic pleasure. Because official Catholic teaching, basing itself on so-called natural law, condemns any interference in the biological cycle of conception, or any use of sexuality outside its formally procreative potential, we are doubly outcast: we love our own sex, so our erotic pleasures, which become ends in themselves, are nonutilitarian from a strictly reproductive viewpoint; and, because we behave as such, we profoundly and dramatically challenge the heterosexual infrastructure of normalcy. We subvert the self-image of the church as Mother and Bride. These are powerful concepts profoundly anchored in the claims of heterosexual homogeneity, claims developed and refined by both Saint Paul and Saint Augustine in their theological thinking and writing, and echoed by their successors down through the centuries. Such claims, amazingly enough, continue to be made.

It wasn't always like this. There was a time when both men were rebel souls. Paul, or Saul of Tarsus as he was known before his Damascus conversion, was a Jewish orthodox believer who persecuted Christians, then seen as members of a breakaway sect of Judaism. He held the cloaks of those who stoned the deacon Stephen, the first official Christian martyr. He was, in fact, a type of religious fanatic who believed strongly in the righteousness of his cause and purpose. Some might indeed claim that he brought the same sense of fanaticism and single-minded devotion to his defense and establishment of Christianity as a universal religion in its own right, and that, if it weren't for his forceful personality, the other apostles and disciples would certainly not have had the vision and sheer gumption to do so. From obsessed persecutor, Paul became a staunch defender of the faith, fundamentally not that much of a shift in perspective. His persecutions, simply enough, assumed a different shape: immoral people and, sadly, women.

Augustine's story is equally dramatic. A free-thinking philosopher and rebel in his youth, his conversion, described so beautifully and powerfully in that quintessentially psychoanalytical modern work, *Confessions,* marks not only a personal shift, but also one for Christendom as a whole. This was a man who had lived unmarried with a woman and had fathered a son out of wedlock. Here was a man who spoke of the death of his friend in hauntingly homoerotic terms. Yet when he chose Christianity — for it was nothing, if not a rational choice — an acute and exaggerated sense of guilt entered, not only his own life, but the entire edifice of Christian belief. Augustine is the father of original sin. The manner in which he judges his past faults in *Confessions* (a particularly telling example is that of the adolescent theft of apples from an orchard) strikes one as being overly critical and fastidious. Augustine inserts into Christian theology a radical disjunction between matter and spirit, thus tainting, with serious and lasting results, all of Western culture, even though he himself fought against this type of thinking during his lifetime. He also condemns women to the role of temptress, a conduit of sin in an already diseased and helpless world. Augustinian teaching on this question can lay claim to being one of the more guilty sources of theological sexism.

Both are, in a strange and telling way, men's saints. Both possessed forceful and domineering personalities, each very much a product of his own patriarchal time and culture. Both remain very much suited to a male-dominated institutional church. The theological edifices that they constructed reflect a male-centered, heterosexual view, not only of reality as such, but also of the nature of the godhead and of sexual morality. Both saints have a difficult time with the messiness of human bodies, though Paul can be hauntingly beautiful in his poetic musings on the links between marriage and the spiritual character of the church. Both believe unfailingly in a God who is severe and judgmental, masculine in his person and in his thinking, an authority figure above and beyond human contingency. Though both may at times speak elegantly of divine love, this love remains that of a distant father for a rebellious child, of a stern though careful shepherd for his wandering flock. It is essentially a man's view of the world.

My first encounter with the thought of Saint Augustine was not theological, but rather political. It was in the context of an undergraduate course on Roman, medieval, and Renaissance political philosophy. We read excerpts from his famous *City of God.* I do not recall much of it, though I do remember being impressed with the airtight logic and attraction of his argumentation. I had a similar response when I first encountered the argumentation of Thomas Aquinas in a course on the "philosophy of man" taught by an old-fashioned Jesuit who believed in the virtues of rote, with the subtle though persistent help of a wandering pointer. There is something re-assuring though slightly scary about thinkers, religious or not, who seek to provide a total explanation for everything. I found Augustine's political philosophy ultimately to be an exercise in self-serving clericalism, though no doubt utopian enough to excite the imagination. I just wasn't sure I wanted to be a citizen of such a pure and perfect City of God. Something was telling me I would never fit in, try as I may.

Pauline thought, on the other hand, I grew up with. Because it has always been part of the Catholic liturgy — the famous epistles from Saint Paul read before the gospel — it only made sense that I should absorb it by osmosis. We all know, almost by heart, some of these texts. In the 1960s, when the Age of Aquarius was dawning and love was afoot in the land, I was especially taken with the "Love is patient; love is kind" bit. This epistle still moves me, though I am now understandably somewhat more jaded about the virtues of selfless love as a lasting force for social or cultural change. Yet Christian thought would be nothing without the words and dogmas of the rebellious Paul to circumscribe it. The life and influence of Jesus of Nazareth would have remained that of an itinerant and sectarian backwater Jewish mystic were it not for Saint Paul's universal vision of the promise of Christian salvation. As with Augustine's City, how-ever, Paul's vision does not really apply to me, and I cannot fully lay claim to its promise. I remain an outcast in this world, a lover of men, an abomination to the church that he was so instrumental in found-ing. If we follow his logic, I should be put to death, as other queer men down through the ages have been, all in the name of religious and moral truth.

In the Church of Santa Maria del Popolo in Rome, Michelangelo
Caravaggio painted two large canvases. One is of the martyrdom of
Saint Peter, who was crucified upside down. The other depicts the
conversion of Saint Paul on the road to Damascus. Both are strikingly
engaging. As the two central personages of the early church — the
first representing continuity; the second, change — it would make
theological and political sense for the painter to place them side-by-
side, facing each other in the small church. In the case of Saint Peter's
crucifixion, the image shows the cross of the Prince of the Apostles
being hoisted upward by three anonymous men pulling on a rope.
The painting is a study in motion. You can almost feel the cross being
lifted from right to left by the push-and-pull movement of the faceless
executioners. Peter's gaze is tired. He gently seems to be welcoming
his deliverance from the arduous duties of church government. This
is quite a human Peter, uncertain and puzzled to the very end, never
totally sure of his calling or his master, a study in human weakness
and vacillation surpassed and glorified.

The painting of Paul's conversion is an awkward work. The center
of focus is not the blinded apostle, but rather the horse from which
he has presumably just fallen. The animal occupies fully one-half of
the picture, its massive flank and legs almost crushing the fallen rider.
A barelegged assistant attempts to hold down the frightened animal.
The heavenly light of conversion is reflected on the animal's body,
hitting a Saint Paul lying flat on his back, his arms stretched heavenward, his legs parted and opened out, one knee upraised. He is dressed
in a military uniform, his helmet to the side of his head. An unusual
element is the almost erect nipple that protrudes from the left side
of his torso. The face is young, though bearded. His hair appears fine
and curly. His eyes are closed in an attitude of willful submission.
The mouth, slightly open, seems to speak words of supplication. It
invites kissing. This is a Paul literally being seduced by the Christian
god he has so fanatically and systematically persecuted. A frankly

homosexual artist, Caravaggio knew full well the subtle import of his visual message. Religious conversion is very much like being ravaged by a possessive and demanding lover.

My encounter with this wondrous work brought the image of sodomy powerfully to mind. Saint Paul has assumed the position: lying on his back, his arms and legs open to the unknown lover, ready to embrace the body of his aggressor. His lit face does not show pain or fear. Rather, its sensually open mouth appears to welcome and desire the mystical body of the unknown god. This is a Paul in whom I could believe: a Paul as far removed from the doctrinaire and orthodox theologian as can be, a Paul freely enjoying the almost erotic experience of spiritual illumination, a passive and vulnerable Paul; not a persecutor, but a lover. It echoes the graceful image of an equally silent victim sacrificed to assuage the wrath of another distant, voracious god, and whose followers the smitten Paul had himself sought out to kill and maim. This portrait of an arrogant Saint Paul in the throes of being spiritually ravished by the divine light speaks eloquently of the possibility of mutation and change in human lives. Conversion does not only happen on the stony road to Damascus. It can throw you flat on your back in the most unexpected of circumstances, the better to enter and possess you hungrily.

Gay men resonate quite naturally to such an image of an eroticized conversion. In some significant ways, the coming out process parallels this existential spiritual moment. From being swiftly and suddenly seized with an urge to change one's horizons and focus, to the impulsive euphoria of a new lifestyle, to the discovery of fresh values: both gay men's and Paul's experiences denote shifts in paradigm, a repositioning of one's very identity and purpose. Though few comings out are as dramatic or sudden as a religious conversion — largely because they are a continuous, never-ending process of smaller moments of truth — they can be risky, life-altering business, as spiritual choices often are in a highly secularized culture. Most of us are still coming out, obliged as we are to play a variety of personal and professional roles at different moments in our lives. I wonder at times what Paul's conversion was all about. It surely had to do with a certain confident acknowledgment and acceptance of the man Jesus as Messiah. But was Paul perhaps going further? Was he, in fact, coming out as a Christian? He had frequented and persecuted the sect so often that he may have discovered himself really and irrevocably to be one of them, much like the rabid homophobe who awakens to an unexpected awareness and acceptance of his own repressed homosexuality. Such abrupt transitions might appear puzzling and slightly suspicious, but, for the believer, the grace of the Spirit knows no bounds.

The fundamental problem with Saint Paul lies in the fact that, as with any convert, he was much too sure of himself. The fanaticism of a newfound faith replaced the more judicious and jaded outlook of the seasoned persecutor. In fact, one should question Paul's statements with respect to homosexuality. They are so completely outrageous that they raise fundamental questions about the man's own sexuality, cultural differences and interpretations aside. Some say that, in his writings, he was actually condemning various forms of idolatrous behavior, rather than homosexuality *per se*. But to lump same-sex erotic behavior together with the religious worship of idols reveals a serious moralistic flaw, a severe judgmental lapse. It underscores the illusions of certainty and superiority that inhabit the newly converted mind. It bespeaks arrogance, the curse of the fanatic.

Most images of Saint Augustine show him in a severe ecclesiastical pose as bishop of Hippo, miter on head and crosier in hand, ever ready to declaim on some obscure point in theology or do intellectual battle with some renegade heretical group. Images of Saint Paul are not as pompous (he is never shown in the guise of a bishop), though both men share a similar look of off-putting severity and grave purpose. Though Paul's conversion could be considered a staple of religious art — the more dramatic, the better — Augustine's is seldom, if ever, depicted. It would be quite difficult, if not impossible, to portray an act of rational and deliberate choice. For that is what Augustine's conversion was: a slow, methodical, considered turning to the Christian God. It was the conversion of an intellectual. Yet strangely enough, it was also the conversion of someone who had just fallen in love. The famous passage from his *Confessions* is most telling in this regard.

> Late have I loved you, fairness so ancient and so new; late have I loved you! For behold you were within me and I was without, and there did I seek you. In my unfair state I rushed heedlessly among the beautiful things of your creation. You were with me, but I was not with you. Those things kept me far from you, though they had no existence except in you. You called and cried aloud, and forced open my deafness. You sent forth your beams and shone, and chased away my blindness. You breathed fragrance, and I drew in my breath and now do sigh after you. I tasted, and now do hunger and thirst after you. You touched me, and I burn for your peace.[21]

These words shimmer with an honest and touching beauty. They tell the story of a long game of seduction: one lover ceaselessly chasing and pining for the other, until the helpless second can no longer resist the repeated advances of his companion. The poetry of the words and images opens up deep spaces for the emergence of an erotic language properly suited to the spiritual experience of conversion. Humans have no other way to express such a life-shattering moment of persuasive enticement. For us, love is the most potent manifestation of who and what we are as persons. Love makes us most fully and perfectly human. In this haunting passage from Augustine, it is God who becomes the hungry and desperate lover, ever inviting the haunted soul to taste, and hear, and feel the divine presence at the very heart of creation. We can all translate this feeling into our commonly human experience of falling in love. When we do, the world becomes, as it were, a magical, illuminated place. Everything feels, or looks, or tastes, or sounds as though it were charged with a sharper, purer light and meaning. Augustinian theological discourse, despite its heavy, magisterial tone, can also blaze with the delicate grace of a sublimely divine touch.

Augustine can be equally eloquent on friendship. He recounts how, in his early twenties, when he "went on seducing and being seduced, deceiving and being deceived in various desires,"[22] he had a close friend who suddenly died following a recurrent fever. He is heartbroken. The *Confessions* goes on for several pages about this sad experience. One especially poignant passage reads:

> At this sorrow my heart was utterly darkened. Whatever I looked on was death. My native country was a torture to me, and my father's house a strange unhappiness. Whatever I had been used to share with him became, without him, a cruel torment. My eyes sought him everywhere, but he was not there. I hated all places because he was not in them, nor could they any more say to me, "Look, he is coming," as they had when he was alive and absent from me. I became a great puzzle to myself, and asked my soul why she was so sad, and why she so disquieted me; but she did not know what to say in reply. If I said "Trust in God," she did not obey me, for good reason: that most dear friend whom she had lost was better and more real than the Manichee phantasm in which I bid her to trust. To me nothing was sweet but tears; they succeeded my friend as the love of my heart.[23]

On first reading, a passage such as this one — or the entire story of this friendship, for that matter — strikes one as unusual and out-of-place in the context of the Augustinian canon. Though one can only surmise on the exact nature of this deep friendship, it would be naive and especially foolish, I would suggest, not to understand and attempt to explain the relationship as a homoerotic one. The intensity of the emotions and the vulnerability with which Augustine writes about them leave little if any room for some other form of interpretation. For Saint Augustine to have a close, intimate relationship with another man would not have been entirely out of character for him at this stage in his life. He admits to "being seduced in various desires," and he was notorious, as he himself writes, for his licentious ways. His feelings for his dead friend are couched in the words of a man in love, not a dispassionate, friendly love, but the hurting, hungry love born of an erotic desire for the other. On reading this passage, I am sad for Augustine. His loss is obviously deep, though he later questions such affections as being "unclean." I am especially sad, however, that he should so clearly reject and demonize bodily desire in his subsequent theological writings. For a man who had so much enjoyed the comforts of human flesh and want, then to turn around and dismiss it all so neatly, strikes me as the most pernicious form of self-hatred. It is even more sad that this hatred turned on us all.

I use "sad," but I really should say that I resent it. In the case of Augustine, one has the constant and eerie impression that one is the innocent bystander victim of his own exaggerated sense of guilt about his life and supposed sexual transgressions. This guilt underpins his entire theological legacy to Catholic Christianity. We are all paying for his reputed faults, several of which raise serious questions about whether they should even be considered as such. Augustine was a man given to extremes: from being the hedonist, he moved to being the perfect religious convert. In so doing, he rejected everything that had gone before, including all the human relationships, in fact, that had been his support and solace. Perhaps as a form of therapeutic exercise, he then went on to cast his influential teachings in the imagery and tones of the bodily and sexual guilt he was feeling, and the dangerous spirit-matter, world-heaven split entered

Christian thought. Roman Catholic sexual morality since that day has been marked by the excessive puritanism and guilt that was Saint Augustine's, whether it be its pronouncements on women, same-sex desire, or human reproduction.

But enough is enough. Why should our lives be subject to the manipulative and destructive touches of guilt-ridden theologians and closeted clerics? Why should their claimed power over us and our bodies be as the church states it to be? Why should we even listen? Of course, many of us are fast refusing to do so, and this brings hope and promise to us all. It is a well-known fact that one of the most potentially serious and damaging things happening to Catholicism at the present time is the radical breach that has emerged over decades between official teaching on sexual morals (influenced heavily by the narrow confines of Augustinian thinking) and their timely rejection by significant numbers of lay believers. People can no longer allow themselves to be spoken down to as though they were children unable and unwilling to express their sexuality as fully mature and responsible human beings. So when the current pope, in his aged obsessions, chastises the "selfishness" and "indifference" of believers, or refers to this time as "the culture of death," he sadly misreads the presence of the Spirit in history. His empty and disconnected pronouncements simply serve to undermine further, in many people's minds, an increasingly discredited and ultimately irrelevant Catholic sexual theology.

The question we must ask ourselves, with increasing urgency, is why we should even bother to listen to the church? And this does not simply have to do with Catholic sexual teaching. It cuts across all aspects of contemporary Catholic culture, from the hierarchy and its protected male clerical culture down to Sunday mass in the local parish. Perhaps we do indeed turn more conservative as we get older, or perhaps we simply become more unwilling to accept mediocrity and hypocrisy. I do not go to Sunday mass as often as I should. The urge is simply not there. Sometimes, I feel guilty about this, but then I ask myself why I should bother. Mine is an urban working-class parish in decline. The most recent priority of its young pastor was the media-heavy papal visit to Toronto for World Youth Day. Others throughout the year include the scouting movement, Bible study and prayer for the under-thirties, and a shelter for homeless kids in the church basement. These are all worthy causes, but where do I find myself reflected as an adult, and especially as a gay man? This is the same pastor who preached against homosexuality on gay pride Sunday some years ago. When I do go to mass, there is no mystery or reverence in the ceremony, simply monotone guitar songs, silly slogans on the walls, and interminable and meaningless kisses of peace. Contemporary Catholic culture is tacky in the extreme, increasingly disconnected from the concerns and priorities of an adult world, trying too hard to be relevant in a child's fantasyland. I feel as though the church has given up on me.

I'm not sure what the voices of Paul and Augustine would tell me. I guess they would tell me to shut up, sit down, and simply follow unquestioningly the teachings (*their* teachings) and the rituals of my church. Or are those the uses to which their voices are put by others, by the church hierarchy itself? One of the very real dilemmas when it comes to understanding and even appreciating the influence and import of these two "manly" saints in my life, in our lives as gay men, is how much one can love and desire the persecutor, the homophobe, the perennial straight man. We have all struggled with this. We have all secretly desired the class bully who calls us sissy, the muscular athlete who taunts us, the heterosexual man who lets himself be sucked, but only because this proves he's not really gay. This is the dangerous territory of attraction to the dark powers that seek to humiliate us and even, at times, deny our existence. Though there really are no rules of attraction, the image of our opposites can be strangely and erotically enticing.

Much of my response to these two saints has to do with a process of seduction by the bully. Though they consistently reaffirm my supposedly corrupt nature, though they are used by churchly powers to condemn and ostracize me, though they call me sinner, ungodly, and morally unfit for salvation, I still respond in awe to their forceful, savagely domineering personalities. I still want the straight persecutor to desire me, and perhaps also to let himself be seduced by me. This irrational pull toward what repels us, toward the radically and frighteningly other, often lies at the dark center of erotic desire. Perhaps I also detect glimmers of hope. In Augustine's passionate declaration of love and sorrow for his dead friend, and in his erotic reading of God's unstinting need and mad hunt for the lapsed sinner, I hear the soft whisper of homoerotic lust. In the vigorously invasive beauty and ferocious delight of Paul's sudden conversion, I sense a man reborn to the hidden possibilities of his loving human nature, which definitely includes the manly and handsome Jesus of Nazareth. In my own grappling with the secret urges and confines of gay polyamory, as well as in my adoration of the erect, phallic god, I conjure up the dark and pliant forces which the Pauline and Augustinian church has long told me to reject for fear of losing my eternal soul. And I spit out a resounding "no." I have thankfully found my soul.

I like to imagine a conversation between Saints Paul and Augustine in the misty hereafter. I hope they spend eternity blaming each other for their common sins.

Blessed Paul and Augustine, doctors and defenders of the faith, men of integrity, architects of an inhuman theology of sexuality, you have done us harm. We are grateful for the beauty and passion of your words, but we also pray that our common brotherly love will shield us from their poison. You have been misused to condemn us and our desires for the affections and bodies of other men. We think you understood us. We need you now to stand with us. Inspire and motivate the leaders of our faith to see the hatred they spread against us in your name. Convert them as you were once converted. Be our strength, our bold and born-again guides. Amen.

SIX

The Ugandan and North American Martyrs

IN THE JULY–AUGUST 1968 issue of the magazine *Eucharist* published by the Blessed Sacrament Fathers, the religious order to which I belonged, in an article on the Martyrs of Uganda, one can read:

> Twenty-two men were canonized by Pope Paul VI as saints and martyrs of the Church on October 18, 1964. These Ugandans, most of them pages at the court of King Mwanga in 1884, died amid torture in defense of their faith. The principal occasion for the king's persecution was the steadfast refusal of his Christian pages to cooperate in sin.[24]

"Cooperate in sin." The expression is slightly quaint, conjuring up uncertain and sordid images of some excessive, nameless behavior. Yet to anyone raised a Catholic at a certain period in time — the 1950s, for example — this "sin," this fault can be none other than sexual. For in the Catholic worldview, almost all true sins are, by definition, sexual ones. Why else would the act remain so unspecified in this passage, and why would cooperation, thereby implying more than one person, necessarily be involved? No doubt about it, the pages were being asked to participate in some sexual activity. But with the king, a man? Or with the members of his entourage? Could it be? Yes. Sodomy. The great unspoken, abominable vice. The Ugandan martyrs were put to death because they refused to engage in same-sex acts, presumably as the passive recipients of some kingly or otherwise upper-class ardor. As with Maria Goretti, they were martyrs, not necessarily to the faith, but to what they understood as their own bodily purity. Which raises the far more tantalizing possibility that, before choosing to say "no," they had, at some point earlier, said "yes," and presumably enjoyed it. Young queer saints indeed.

Another hagiographic text, this one considerably more direct in its references to the king's desires and the responses of his young page boys:

And they will not submit to the king's vices. The latter is constantly solliciting [*sic*] his pages, especially the youngest ones. Pagans and Moslems dare not resist him. But the young Christians pluckily refuse his advances. They are well aware that their life is at stake. But it is the pure who will see God, and they wish to see God.

It is over them particularly that the storm will break.[25]

This fragment is interesting at several different levels. Apart from the standard rhetoric about the vices and solicitations of "dirty old men," it raises the bugaboo of pedophilia, and it echoes the ancient and very pejorative Christian equation of this sexual practice with the followers of Islam, but also with so-called African pagans. It reaffirms bodily purity as a central motif in the spiritual lives of Catholic youth. Perhaps most significantly, it makes explicit the connection between same-sex practices and the outbreak of the persecutions.

The story of the Martyrs of Uganda (Saints Charles Lwanga and Companions) can only be properly understood from the perspective of the nineteenth-century intersections of race, sexuality, and colonial expansion on the African continent.[26] These saints are considered the protomartyrs of Black Africa, which means that the account of their deaths stands as "the founding narrative of

Christianity" on African soil. Strangely enough — or perhaps not — this is a story constructed on male same-sex desire, specifically the "treacherous" vice of sodomy, and its subsequent denial and punishment. The legend of the Martyrs, "the uprooting of same-sex practice on the Dark Continent," is really about black bodies as dangerous and hypersexualized entities, a typically Western mythos, and the need for the white Christian conquerors to control and discipline them, also a standard paradigm of colonial thinking. The sacred text of the Martyrs of Uganda, at its heart, recounts "a sexual story"; and even though it is "a canonized story," it remains "a story denied."

The denial functions at two levels. First, it touches upon the sensitive and much debated issue of homosexuality in African cultures, and, more contemporaneously, its place within notions of black manhood, specifically African American. It is interesting to note, for example, that King Mwanga is reputed to have learned same-sex behavior from outsiders, again a typical scapegoating strategy in response to sexual difference. In its October entry for the Ugandan Martyrs, *Butler's Lives of the Saints* makes the following gratuitous and totally incredulous comment in referring to Mwanga: "He is said to have learned these practices from traders from the north, since they were not common among his own people."[27] What is the implied assumption? That no true black male, especially one who is a leader, can be, by nature or by choice, desiring of other men, and, moreover, that such unnatural and suspect behavior is something imported from elsewhere, brought in by foreigners as a way of corrupting the pristine quality of the home culture. It is the same argument once heard from the Soviet leadership, and occasionally put forth today by that of Communist China. The denial of same-sex desire and behavior, whatever the social, political, or theological context, only serves to accentuate its cultural attendance.

A second denial has to do with theology and religious power. If you canonize the sodomites, then your efforts are vindicated. If you can claim that they died as martyrs because they refused to succumb to corrupt and lascivious ways, thereby reaffirming their belief in Christian virtue and their identity as Christians, then your missionary enterprise has not been in vain. And so, you don't necessarily highlight the same-sex dynamic at the center of their story. You speak of not "cooperating in sin." You gloss over the sexual details of their former lives, or you claim their executioner was not really himself, or you might even transform them into saints, and prototypical ones at that. The power of religious recuperation and reappropriation is remarkable indeed. Though the story of the Ugandan Martyrs is, in part, exemplary of the clash between Western Christendom and African native traditions, it is even more illustrative of a customary Catholic silence on male same-sex desire. How better to ensure the silent cooperation of these potentially problematic saints, and, by extension, that of their devotees, than by declaring them to be full members of the heavenly host? How better, therefore, to hide this desire that is at the very heart of Catholic clerical culture? It is indeed remarkable and somewhat poetic in its justice that the Ugandan Martyrs should have been canonized by Pope Paul VI, who was himself reputed to be a homosexual.[28] Though this does not in any way detract from the genuine sanctity and worthiness of the Martyrs themselves, it does beg some rather interesting questions with respect to who gets to decide sainthood, and why.

But raising sodomites, homosexuals, and other queers, whatever their age, to the glory of the altars can be risky business. The real text always manages to seep through, and the theologians and hagiographers remain hard-pressed to try and contain it. A fair number of the twenty-two Ugandan Martyrs were, after all, directly in the employ of the monarch, many as pages, and several had no doubt been willing partners in any number of sexual escapades with him or officials at his court. It is simply not good enough to claim, as though one were writing a brand of revisionist history, that such practices "were not common," or even that the Martyrs were and remained virginal. Such practices were obviously common enough to be a cause of concern among the Christian converts, and it is possible that servicing the king was considered a normal part of the routine duties and responsibilities of a serious and hard-working page boy. Were they chosen specifically because of their good looks? Possibly. Whatever the facts, many were killed initially because they became the unwilling partners in some homoerotic fixation and dance of power. Whether or not they may have died for the faith remains an open, if perhaps not an irrelevant, question.

What theology may choose to skirt, fantasy will complete. And so, when a gay man kneels and prays to the Holy Martyrs of Uganda, he is venerating his own flesh and blood, his own desires, his own identity. He is reclaiming the witness of these saints as just one further example of what an oppressive heterosexist system can do to queers. By minimizing, dismissing, erasing, and ultimately denying the real grounds for their death, churchly and other types of officials want to turn the Ugandan Martyrs into safe and well-contained saints. More seriously yet, it is very possible that some of these Martyrs were lovers of men, or that they had emerging same-sex desires. Perhaps some of them were partners in real life, perhaps older men with younger boys, given that their age span went from the mid-forties to the early teens. They were sexual beings, some of them no doubt active and deliberate in expressing their need for other men. The subtext of their martyrdom is that of desire: a desire spiritualized and sanctified, but also a desire burning with the love and grace of homoerotic need demonized and cut short.

In *The Invention of Sodomy in Christian Theology,* Mark D. Jordan recounts and analyzes the hagiographic legend of the pubescent Saint Pelagius, an Iberian Christian saint of the tenth century sometimes used in Christian anti-Muslim polemic.[29] The motifs surrounding his life, death, and subsequent cult are replete with images and whispers of same-sex desire, and they parallel very closely the typical story of the Ugandan Martyrs: beautiful boys, lascivious rulers, requests for sexual pleasure, rejection on the grounds of purity and faith, and the eventual killing of beautiful boys. In fact, as Jordan points out, the story of Pelagius is *all about* same-sex desire, for its key actors are male. He writes:

> Pelagius knows the customs of same-sex desire, and he plays with that desire itself when he strips before the king in order to spurn him. He spurns the king as well in what he says. When Pelagius proclaims that he "cherishes Christ," when he chooses to die or to suffer "for Christ," when he invokes no one other than "the Lord Jesus Christ," he is speaking the name of his true love in the face of a rival. For the king, the choice facing Pelagius seems to be between pleasure and pain, between his own gracious self and a fictive god. For Pelagius, the choice seems to lie between ephemeral and permanent pleasure, between an earthly and a heavenly king, between an imperfect lover and a perfect one. The story of the martyrdom is, through Pelagius's eyes, the story of a passionate triangle in which all the parties are male. *He does not deny same-sex love so much as he vindicates it by choosing Christ as his lover.*[30]

As is the case with the Martyrs of Uganda, Pelagius's choice is against one male lord and master, and for another. But it is precisely in choosing the favors and love of a man, though he be that other, that the young saints, both Iberian and Ugandan, claim their own same-sex desires. They do not repudiate or deny these desires, so much as celebrate and vindicate them. Their martyrdom is really only the story of a protracted and gracious seduction, one culminating in eternal union with their chosen lover and bridegroom. The text may have been "written out" of their lives by church powers, but it never went away.

When I first heard about these new black saints in the euphoria of the civil rights movement of the 1960s, I was excited that the church had finally taken what appeared to be a bold step for racial equality. I certainly do not recall any hushed mention of sodomy and other perverse practices, nor did I yet possess the intellectual sophistication needed to tease out the historical links between race, gender, and colonialism. For me, they were simply the first black African martyr-saints, nothing less and certainly nothing more. But coming at them today, I am quite amazed at my response to them: a response of affection and sympathy, but one also tainted by anger and frustration. For once again, our queer history has been deliberately written out; our story, only half-told. The Holy Martyrs of Uganda, more than any of the others in this collection, with the possible exception of Saint Sebastian, are truly iconic gay saints, in their spiritual grandeur as in their silent desires.

Some two hundred years earlier, half a world away from the hot intensity of the African sun, lost in the deep snows of the North American continent, another group of protomartyrs died for the faith at the hands of Iroquois warriors. Known as the North American Martyrs (and sometimes as the Canadian Martyrs), they were eight Jesuit missionaries (Saints Jean de Brébeuf and Companions). In French Canadian historical lore, these martyr-saints occupy a rather prestigious and predominant place.[31] They became a prime symbolic representation of ultramontane claims over the Catholic soul of French Canada, and of the missionary zeal and religious single-mindedness of its founders. Partly an ideological construct, they also embodied Jesuit worldly spirituality at its most confident and its most altruistic. What is particularly striking, however, about the devotional cult to these North American clerical saints is the repeated, detailed, and very graphic emphasis on the specific forms of their martyrdom. Sadistic images of torture abound in their iconography, as though this were a way of heightening the intensity of one's veneration of them. All this colorful pain and humiliation is intensely tied up with the negative stereotyping of native peoples as cruel and heartless savages, thereby serving rather crude historical ends. For me, on the other hand, it was not at all like this. The Iroquois excited me, in more ways than I understood.

When I was a child and young adolescent, the Canadian television corporation would often present historical dramas based on the history of New France, the period prior to the British Conquest of 1759 when France ruled what is now Quebec. These dramas, generally very well acted and directed, presented a somewhat idealized view of the French era in North America. It was a typically "good guy–bad guy" sort of history, with not very many shades of gray in between. This was grand and glorious adventure, and certainly exciting enough to quicken a young boy's pulse. But what quickened my pulse above all were the proverbial bad boys of French Canadian history, the almost-naked, muscular, smooth-bodied Iroquois warriors. What a dangerous, titillating pleasure it was to watch them boldly threaten the safety of the settlers, or run through the forest in hot pursuit of an enemy they would later scalp. They were invariably well-proportioned, tall, bald, and covered only in a loincloth under which I imagined unspeakable delights, or at times simply a well-hung appendage. I very much wanted to be their prisoner, if only as a means of gaining intimate access to the sexual frenzy in which I imagined they lived their lives on a regular basis, and consequently become a part of it.

Mine was certainly the fetishistic gaze of a Westernized boy, feeding hungrily on the stock images of exotic Indians and "others" as projections of sexual panic and desire. As with the classic figure of the Roman gladiator in my imagination, the Iroquois warrior occupied a strategic and dominant space. He was safe because historical, but dangerous because so very desirable. He both attracted and repelled. He was also the executioner of those most holy Jesuit martyrs. Like the devil, this made him doubly suspect and hazardous. But like the devil, he was far sexier and attractive than his good and saintly antagonists. The Iroquois warrior troubled me. I wanted him, but I was equally aware of the strange cruelties he was said to inflict, and I felt slightly guilty about my hidden and unspoken desires for him. On the other hand, the foolhardy black robes, as the natives called the Jesuit missionaries, never really impressed me too much. They seemed slightly imperialistic and insipid, fawning after martyrdom as one does after some forbidden treat. My Iroquois warrior was actually doing them a favor by torturing them to death. He was turning them into saints. In many ways, he could do no wrong, because he was so sexy.

His sexiness, though totally foreign to me in my uncertain prepubescent fixation, functioned as an escape valve. It somehow lessened the visceral fear and apprehension that his persona, as historically fictionalized and romanticized as it was, unconsciously brought out in me. Or rather, it played on them. For in actual fact, it was the *frisson* of fear that made the Iroquois warrior sexy, even though the skimpy loincloth and the broad shoulders played undeniably large parts in the equation. The sexual allure of the slightly dark and perilous, of the unfamiliar and the abnormal, can turn us all into willing and far more submissive partners in the erotic game than we are often prepared to admit. As can, for that matter, a wonderfully brawny pair of thighs. And brawny the Iroquois warriors certainly were! I have often wondered why they were invariably shown this way. Part of it may have been ethnographically correct, and part of it certainly served the function of ideological recuperation and projection, but the other reason must have had to do with the desires of the creators of these images. When I so avidly and uncritically ingested such images, I was sharing in the needs, wants, and appetites of these unknown men, thereby touching what was common between us. I had no concept what that might mean, even less that we were homosexuals, but the beginnings of shared desires and identities were very much present, and, in retrospect, gladly so.

In some important ways, I do not think that the Iroquois warrior would have been so desirable in my mind had he not stood in a necessary symbiotic relationship with his saintly victims. As is the case with the dynamic between popular and formal religion, for example, so the martyr needs his or her executioner, as much as the executioner needs his (rarely her) martyr, in order that both can understand and properly fulfill their roles. It is the henchman who creates the martyr, and, for the believer, who is as much a central part of the religious drama as the saint. To the henchman, who must often remain anonymous except in the case of powerful men, can be affixed any number of human foibles, wants, and even qualities. They can be lustful or voracious, stupid or authoritarian, mindless or astute, beautiful or needy, bit players or major villains. What they are not, however, is negligible entities or nonperformers in the martyrdom scene. In the devotional strategy of the believer, veneration of the saintly victim invariably includes the hapless instrument of divine grace, the martyr's killer.

It is torture that still defines the cult of the North American martyrs, and I would argue that it is the executioners, not the saintly victims, who are the real motif and legend of the story. The tortures were gruesome indeed, tied up in complex ways with Iroquois beliefs about spirits, power, courage, and the afterlife. Among others: the pulling of nails and hair, the flaying and burning of skin, death by tomahawk, by red hot irons, by boiling water, and the eating of the roasted flesh of the victims. Simply recounting this well-worn, sad litany of cruelties perpetuates the sacred myth of the Martyrs and the equally well-engrained myth of gratuitous and meaningless Iroquois violence. It is interesting that I am able to repeat, almost by rote, these various forms of torment. It demonstrates quite unmistakably how much the seminal narrative of the North American Martyrs, in all its gory details, was, at one time, a major part of the collective heritage and consciousness of French Canadian society. Those who were blamed for having inflicted such sufferings were pivotal to this heritage, albeit in an unnecessarily diabolical way. I, for one, did not really mind their role as demons, though I resented the blame, because these anonymous and bewitching executioners were fodder for my dreams.

The story and legend of the North American Martyrs resonates with an especially strong sadomasochistic theme, at once culturally and spiritually normative: the former, in how it has been deployed as an instrument of clerical and religious institutional power; the latter, in that it exhibits, once again and rather forcefully, the perennial ties that bind spiritual ecstasy and physical suffering. Both sets of Martyrs, the Ugandan and the North American, also blur sexual and racial lines, though each further reinscribes a particular Catholic canonical text centered on suffering and persecution. In both cases, the playing out of the drama centers around the encounter of an expansionist Western religion with the cultures of indigenous peoples, and the fatal consequences that inevitably follow for both sets of protagonists. These are also "feminized" stories. I was struck, in reading some of the legends around the North American Martyrs, by how the Jesuits were often perceived by native peoples as womanly and subservient, not fully men. In the case of the Ugandan Martyrs, the fear was of "being eaten" culturally by effeminate Christians. The martyrdom scenarios served as opportunities for exorcising masculine anxieties.

The most popular iconographical representation of the North American Martyrs shows two parts to their story: at the bottom of the image, the actual deaths of the eight in collapsed historical time (they died over a seven-year spread), with their executioners, handsome in their half-naked energy, fearlessly going about their pre-ordained task of saint-making; the top three-quarters of the image shows the Jesuit saints in beatific poses, standing and kneeling on a heavenly cloud while delicate angels hand them the palms and crowns of martyrdom. The message is unambiguous: death, and preferably violent death for and in the faith, with the shedding of blood, is the necessary condition for a coveted place in the celestial realm. But there is a further script, this one more subtle by far, that goes something like this: "Contemplate the sadistic tortures inflicted on these Martyrs; let them inspire your devotion and faith; and in contemplating, desire. Desire not only the heavenly reward, but also to partake of their blood-letting and their rapturous gazes. Let the beautiful men who are slicing and cutting them up — the beautiful, savage men — also be your desirable and loving guides, your sensuous gateways to a delightful vision of transcendence." One does not stand very far here from the ecstatic throes of willing body piercing or S-M practitioners, or the blasphemous musings and wicked antics of a certain notorious Marquis de Sade. Nor, for that matter, are we at too great a distance from the spiritual hunger of a John of the Cross or that of a certain Teresa of Avila, both of whom desired fiery divine penetration above all else. As did I, but by the hand (and, hopefully, other fleshy instruments) of my exotic and menacing lover-warrior.

As fate would have it, call it synchronicity, the same issue of *Eucharist* that talks about the Ugandan Martyrs also contains a poem written by a former fellow seminarian, an upperclassmate with whom I recall being particularly close. I had a crush on him, and that is no doubt why I still have a copy of the magazine in question. He was the one who first taught me how to smoke, and I also remember that he would paint and draw. I liked to collect samples of his work. What has stuck with me most of all, however, is an image of him peeing in one of the dormitory urinals. He stood there in his pajamas, hands on hips, and I would peer delicately over the partition, trying to steal a glimpse. He was a sort of older brother to me, a hero, and I carried my secret desire for him like the proverbial flame under a bushel. His poem, obviously the work of a young writer, tells of a mother bringing her son to the foot of the cross on Calvary, a clear reference to the priestly vocation. Its concluding verses:

> we watched
>
> the crowd grew less
>
> soldiers
> tired of play
> were leaving
>
> she put me down
> and to the cross
> led me
>
> under his feet
> I felt his blood
> upon my head
>
> I touched the wood
> I touched the feet
> I touched the blood
>
> I left the hill....
> but never the cross.[32]

Soldiers at play. A man alone on a cross. Caressing his feet. Touching his blood. Feeling the hot liquid cover my head. A sharing of the suffering and the cross. A need to be hung by his side, over him, under him. In these erotically charged Christian images of the crucifixion of Jesus are repeated the anguished sufferings and deaths of martyrs of all time and place, universal and eternal in their witnessing. We summon the Martyrs of the Ugandan jungles and of the North American forests. We proclaim that here stood boys and men full of longing. We name the homoerotic desires of the young page boys, and we declaim the feminine secrets of the fearless black robes. In the calling forth and the writing down, the sifting and the telling of their stories, we stake our rightful claims over their bold lives and heroic legends. Not to please the earthly powers that be, but to honor ourselves and the sacredness of their memory in our lives.

The Jesuits have had a strong influence in my life, both their spirituality and their pedagogy. The Blessed Sacrament Fathers, with whom my heart truly lies, were among the first to spread the cult of the Ugandan Martyrs through their missionary efforts in that country. I abide at the point of convergence of these two traditions. The North American Martyrs will ever be part of my national and cultural landscape. Those who killed them, my fantasy Iroquois warriors, have shaped my erotic self. The Ugandan Martyrs, whom I so much like because they were far queerer than is ever admitted, and for good reason, I keep discovering anew as a source of hagiographic pleasure. Saints are indeed all about discreet and gentle pleasures: pleasures of the body, and pleasures of the spirit. Queer pleasures.

In the heavenly chambers, might it be that Saint Jean de Brébeuf and his companions have caroused with their holy Ugandan brothers, the better to honor and worship them?

Blessed Martyrs of Uganda and North America, men of faith and conviction, bold witnesses for the good, you inspire us by your confidence and your principles. Be by our side. Give us comfort and repose. Grant us, through Jesus, the grace of your vision and your hope. We know that your lives were ones of hidden, secret desires. We know that you took upon yourselves the denials and fears of helpless, desperate churchmen. As your brothers, we want to reaffirm and celebrate who and what you were. We want to reclaim your exemplary spirituality. Touch us gently. Possess us passionately. Forever hold us in your wonderful arms. Amen.

SEVEN

Francis of Assisi

N O OTHER SAINT is as widely revered and respected, fashionable and recognized, appropriated and misunderstood. No other saint crosses such significant ecumenical boundaries, yet no other saint requires such a profound and serious commitment from his followers. Francis of Assisi is without a doubt the most universal of all saints, yet the message of his life still disturbs in its radical simplicity. This is the saint who completely rejected traditional family bonds, lived a life of total and distressing poverty, talked to birds and tamed wild beasts, first invented the Christmas crèche, and first received the marks of the stigmata. He is part myth and legend, part medieval figure with amazing modern appeal, the saint some called the first hippie. He has served as the inspiration for countless religious conversions and the source of a rather impressive body of literary and artistic production. He continues to tower over all other saints, Mary and perhaps Joseph excepted. Francis of Assisi, for some reason, still haunts our very secularized and sadly impoverished religious imagination. That is because Francis is an uncompromising saint. With him, there is little or no gray, only an extreme, literal, and life-shattering reading of the gospel message.

Francis of Assisi is, however, also a wonderfully campy saint. His communities of young brothers living lives of simple poverty, begging for their daily bread, were the very embodiment of cultural rebellion in their time. He himself welcomed members from all social classes, and of all conditions. He communed with nature on a regular basis, and cavorted with animals of all sorts. He decided to reconstruct and thus reclaim abandoned church buildings, infusing them with a new life and purpose. He went around in the habit of a common beggar, caring for outcasts such as lepers. A young man promised to the brilliance of a military and commercial career, he chose instead to reject worldly glory in favor of fashioning a profoundly new way of living out seriously the radical implications of Christ's call to perfection. Part social rebel, part mystic, Saint Francis of Assisi captured, in his person and in his religious legacy, the ambiguities and possibilities of all culturally marginal actors. On the one hand, they introduce into the arena of public discourse new ways of seeing and doing; on the other, they become the powerless victims of their own appeal and popularity. Francis made possible, in his time and in his place, a space for the questioning of empty material values. He also proposed a model of simplicity and nonattachment that continues to resonate clearly and sharply down to this day. But in the process, Francis the saint has become Francis the sugary icon, a holy man with little if any virile appeal, a safe and effeminate angelic creature.

I prefer to imagine a hot, masculine Francis, a man smelling and tasting of manly juices, a rebellious and undisciplined saint surrounded by his band of equally pungent and unruly companions. This Francis is strong and principled, a persistent thorn in the side of both father and church. With his brothers, he creates communities of the dispossessed and the undesirable, places where outcasts can learn to speak with their own voice. This Francis does not care for worldly approval or stature, nor does he abide the ignorance and stupidity of the powerful. This Francis is not afraid of sex. He sees it as the wonderful gift of the Creator that it is, and he rejects the puritanical and antierotic posturings of the sexually frustrated and immature. This Francis sees all of creation as a sacred moment. He does not judge his disciples, including their sexual lives. He does not resent them their special friendships and occasional couplings. Such energy contributes to the vital dynamism of the community's life. Francis does not worry about what others may think.

Francis of Assisi's was a sweetly pampered body, that of the son of a rich businessman, a body rightly destined to assume its place in a world deeply imprinted with masculine privilege. This young and adored male body, relishing to excess the pleasures of life, went to war, returning deeply wounded and broken in its spirit. It became a questioning body, uncertain as to its place in the world, resentful of its marks of indulgence. This beautiful, desirable body walked away naked from its paternal guardian, assuming the outcast status of the dirty, unkempt body. It was a body that worked hard in manual labor, that begged for its food, whose hands cleansed the putrescent wounds of leprosy and caressed the broken limbs of the outcast and the infirm. It was also a body ravaged with lice and fasting, a body slowly transformed into a holy and spiritually receptive vessel. This was the body that received the ultimate mark of grace and Christ-like possession, the stigmata. This was the body that journeyed under threat of danger to the Holy Land, and the body that guided with love and tenderness the destinies and fortunes of its vowed brothers. It became a holy body, given unto others, luminous and even more intensely pleasing and attractive in its vulnerability and fragility. The perfect religious body, the body of saintly desire.

I write about Francis and the others because I have desired their holy bodies, and because their stature as saints has by no means erased their homoerotic attractiveness. I write to leave a trace and a legacy of a queer Catholicism, a religious faith deeply colored by my (and others') same-sex passions. It does make a difference, and it does contribute to the further naming and appropriation of a gay worldview. If we claim the objects of religious devotion simultaneously as objects of erotic desire, then we can also make ours the salvation which they promise, and do so as proud gay men. It was on and through the bodies of these holy men that I and others first found ourselves, that we first tasted the sweet nectar of forbidden love. And it was their sanctified bodies that made our desire the hallowed gift that it became. The bodies of the saints were our training grounds, our first loves, our unlawful rites of passage. When I now write about the holy body of Saint Francis of Assisi — or any of the others, for that matter — I write my own life story and the unspoken, secret stories of all others like me: Catholic "perverts" trained in the sanctified and timeless "perversions" of an intensely homoerotic institution. I speak what cannot or should not be spoken, the better to uncover its truly liberating message.

Some years ago, while visiting Rome for the first time, I took a day trip to Assisi. The town is impressive from afar, sitting as it does atop a small hill. My memories are somewhat vague. I recall the glorious basilica covering Francis's modest first chapel, the truly massive pilgrimage complex, his ragged and holy tunic behind glass, the splendid and luminescent Giotto frescos of his life, the crucifix in the village church that is reputed to have spoken to him, the quiet tranquility of the crooked streets of the medieval town, the crisply preserved and blackened body of his companion, Clare. The one image that remains with me most clearly is that of a large marble statue of Saint Francis enclosed in a garden, holding a bowl in his hands. A dove, which I thought was also made of stone, stood on the brim. To my sudden amazement, however, I saw that it was quietly and beautifully alive, resting near Francis as though it had always belonged there. Perhaps it did. This single moment captured for me the true meaning and incredible richness of Francis of Assisi's sanctity. Even in rigid statuesque form, he was able to summon creation to his side. This is surely the mark of a very powerful, caring saint.

We all like to think of Francis of Assisi as the ultimate rebel. Each generation creates its own Francis, and takes from his character and legacy that which appeals most to its sense of priorities, whether it be his antimaterialism, his simplicity, his closeness to nature. What Francis proposed to a very rich, feudal medieval church was a profoundly new and uncompromising paradigm for understanding the gospel teachings of Jesus. He created fresh ways of understanding relationships and material goods, and the manner in which power, whether religious or secular, should be comprehended and lived out. He blazed new paths, not in any excessively flamboyant manner, but through the touchingly plain example of his life journey and the legacy of his companions. His values proved timeless: poverty, humility, a genuine pleasure in the wonders of creation. In this radical yet deeply disturbing simplicity, Francis of Assisi altered the course of Christian history. He opened new vistas, showing that there are different ways of relating to each other, of ordering our priorities and values, of making sense — just as gay men are now doing.

Some months ago, in preparation for a series of talks on spirituality and sexuality, I read a wonderful book, a rare and real eye-opener. It is an incredibly important book for us as gay men, one that I certainly would like to have written. Though the author, David Nimmons, writes about gay men specifically, his insights and observations carry significant implications for all queer people, and well beyond. Its title: *The Soul beneath the Skin: The Unseen Hearts and Habits of Gay Men.*[33] It is the sort of book that brings hope and purpose back into our too often jaded lives. A work of passionate confidence, it makes one believe even more strongly in the notion of an ephemeral queer touch across time, of a spirit moving through and with us, down and across history and culture. The title is engaging and eloquent in its suggestiveness: that underneath and through our skin, through our erotic lives and desires as gay men, there breathes and moves a greater and more lasting spiritual force, one ever engaged in its marvelous work of cultural change. As gay men, we are, in fact, harbingers of profound and lasting change in masculine culture and, by extension, culture in its universal dimensions.

Nimmons's thesis is not new, though his argumentation certainly is. It is the old observation that we queer folks (in this case, gay men) have a critical role to play in the transformation of human social arrangements and consciousness, precisely because of our difference and marginal status. This key idea goes back to some of our most illustrious ancestors, Edward Carpenter and Harry Hay among others, and even down today to those searching for that intensely problematic and elusive gay gene. It is a mainstay of queer spiritual thinking, the idea that we constitute "a tribe apart," "a chosen breed," "a people contrary." What Nimmons sets out to accomplish, however, is to prove sociologically what has always been a bit of a mystico-philosophical ideal. He does so eloquently and persuasively, *and* you walk away feeling very good about yourself as a gay man and your wider queer community.

In *The Soul beneath the Skin,* Nimmons argues that gay men today are having a profound yet seldom, if ever, acknowledged impact by altering traditional conceptions of masculinity along six different vectors: in public violence, caretaking and volunteerism, sexual desire and intimacy, friendship and relationships generally, relations with women, and notions of public play and bliss. Nimmons goes one crucial step further: not only are gay men altering the rules of the game about what it might mean to be a man, they are also proposing nothing less than a new kind of public ethic, though we regrettably refuse to acknowledge this in our negative obsessions with the sadly superficial trappings of gay culture. In other words, we are fashioning a new type of masculine identity and, perhaps more broadly and significantly, elaborating novel standards for human interaction. One of the more eloquent examples he gives, statistics in hand, is the total lack of violence in our large-scale male-only gatherings, despite the omnipresence of alcohol and drugs. This would never be, and has never been, the case in similar gatherings of heterosexual men. With erotic desire ever simmering beneath the surface, gay men have no desire or interest in hurting each other. If there is violence, it consists of a healthy ritual acting out.

> Queer-inspired practices, from Radical Faerie gatherings to AIDS volunteer buddy teams, shimmer with notions of communal caretaking and altruism. At their best, they recall nothing so much as New Testament teachings of *agape* and *caritas,* male embodiments of service and nurture, nonviolence and gender peace, brotherhood and friendship, all spiced with equal dollops of sexuality and spectacle. Only in this case, the apostles are wearing Calvins or Abercrombie and Fitch...and sometimes not even that. Yet look at the soul beneath the skin, and you see we are rewriting the defaults of what a culture of men can be with and for each other.[34]

One may think that Nimmons is being unduly optimistic or apologetic about gay men and their lifestyles. To a certain extent he may be, though one should hasten to add that this is a refreshing change from all the neoconservative, antierotic dribble we have been fed by some of our more "popular" gay thinkers in recent years. The thing about Nimmons's book is that it is passionate, convincing, joyful, and certainly very eloquent. He asks us to take ourselves and our culture seriously for once. This is indeed a radical, paradigm-shifting challenge, but a very, very necessary one. This is a saintly task. We are prophets and revolutionaries, dangerous subversives and the forerunners of a new cultural ethos. We need to be serious about our calling and our mission. The signs are all around us. We know the profound and lasting impact we are having on human culture. We all know that, together with our feminist colleagues, we are altering, perhaps forever, key notions of God and gender. Most importantly, we are offering our fellow humans an amazing and colorful panoply of erotic choices and possibilities. We are certainly unique in creating, at this time and in this place, some very different and exciting modes of cultural expression, all of which — from our forms of social interaction to our ways of caring for each other — seem to be charting a new course for humans as a whole. I call that sanctity. I call that prophecy. I call that vision. I call us a communion of saints.

Francis of Assisi, in his uncompromising and engaging simplicity, was equally creative as an agent of cultural change in his society. The values he espoused, the modes of charitable expression he proposed, the types of communal relations he lived out, the path of spiritual wholeness he patterned: all these had a lasting influence, not only on a rigid and materialistic Catholicism, but also on the cultural sensibilities of his times. In response to the violent, war-thirsty ethos of masculine privilege, he offered the engaging model of a simple religious brotherhood; against the all-consuming, empty materialism of economic gain and domination, he offered Lady Poverty; against the marginalization of the most despised of a society's outcasts, he offered sanctuary and acts of mercy; against the world-rejecting, rigidly dualistic theology of a feudal church, he offered a glorious relishing in the wonder of creation. His famous Prayer for Peace proposes a fundamental shift in values for all those desiring to live more intensely as Christian believers, but more importantly as humans. At heart, Francis was quite optimistic and hopeful about human nature, and he was extremely positive about the spiritual benefits and inherent goodness of the material world. One of the reasons for his immense popularity across all levels of the religious spectrum stems precisely from his openness to, and celebration of, the worth and beauty of nature and humankind's handiwork.

As with Saint Francis, not the least of the gifts we, as gay men, bring to the wider human family is a revaluation of desire and pleasure, this potent "bliss" that can be a source of such enmity within and outside our communities. Nimmons says that we are simultaneously feared and envied because of it. Michael Bronski asserts the same thing when he claims that it is our drive for nonutilitarian, non-procreative pleasure in its wide multiplicity of forms that apparently poses such a threat, unfounded though it be, to a certain narrowly defined vision of the American national character.[35] Devotion and excess are necessary to a vitally creative spiritual life, to say nothing of a healthy sex life. As gay men, one of the great lessons we have always taught others, and certainly one of the fundamental reasons, I believe, why we are so much disliked in certain quarters, is precisely because we assert the primacy of pleasure to the human experience, particularly unbridled and anarchistic erotic fun. We are a sexual people. It is a gift that we bring. How could it be any other way?

Theologian Mark Jordan speaks perceptively of "redeeming pleasures."[36] It is a wonderful expression, referring at once to the need to redeem or reclaim the notion of pleasure in the Christian moral tradition, but also to those erotic bodily pleasures that are, in and of themselves, meaningful sources of spiritual insight. He argues that our erotic practices can teach us spiritual truths, and, equally, that our spiritual disciplines can teach us about the erotic. If indeed this is the case, and the great mystics have always believed it to be so, then gay men, by virtue of the amorphous quality of their sexual choices, can open our vision to an appreciation for the sweet ambivalence of the sacred, its uniquely diffused, unstable character. In our spiritual lives, all of us have experienced what it means to "wait upon the spirit," and the simultaneously arid and ecstatic feelings it can produce. We joke about the top and bottom thing, about who's active or passive, and we invent strange acronyms for positioning, differentiating, and specializing ourselves, as any personals column in any gay magazine will attest. Though amusing at times, I would suggest that such flexibility and polyvalence in our erotic object-choices and our sexual couplings are truly a wonderful gift of the Creator, reflective of how the Spirit moves and shapes the universe. I have always thought that my openness to an active receptivity, as well as its flip side, makes me uniquely susceptible, as a gay man, to spiritual awakening, for the force of life is both top and bottom: "top" in its beautifully compelling need to possess and make its own; "bottom" in its rich and gentle receptivity to my needs.

What might this dual openness to the life force mean? First, that we understand and value rapture, the total and unconditional merging with the erotic force, from a position of extreme, powerful, and life-asserting vulnerability. This rapture reminds one of ecstatic prayer, of being penetrated by the Spirit, and baptized in the blood of the Lamb; the speaking of tongues *while* talking dirty. Second, that ours, rather than being simply a merging of difference, is all about the resplendence and multiplication of sameness, same flesh become same flesh. Take this holy body, same as yours, and eat of it. This sameness reminds one of the coextensive Father and Son, same male flesh of same male flesh. And thirdly something to do with the attractive power of idolatry and the glory of male images of divine force; of how the religiously inspired masculine body exerts its magic over us; of the magnetic pull of the crucified Christ or the glorious Shiva. It is said that gay men are obsessed with the body. I claim this obsession as a grace. It is really a devotion written in the heavens, an earthly strategy for engagement with the divine force. Phallic worship, for example, has nothing at all to do with the empty and meaningless sucking of male genitalia, and everything to do with an awareness of human desire as a path to spiritual wholeness. It is a discipline. Somehow, I suspect Saint Francis of Assisi would have understood, if perhaps not approved.

For if Francis was anything, he was earthy; not the gentle and angelic figure of the tacky holy cards, but bold and brawny in his spirituality and in his humanity. A man's man, in other words. Or more precisely, a gay man's man. Francis of Assisi, the seducer and the charmer. Francis, the ultimate outsider, the one who, like so many of us, rejected family because they could not understand, and he did not want to be weighed down with their bankrupt values. Francis the visionary, who ultimately stood alone with his Creator, and was pierced by his fiery and bloody wounds as a special sign of divine love and election. Saint Francis of Assisi, the boy wonder who became the saint wonder. Francis, my love, my craving, my compulsion, my sweet man.

As a child, I had a particular fondness for dressing up in costumes with religious overtones. Quite young, perhaps some eight or nine years old, I recall that I liked to play at being a nun, like the white Holy Ghost Sisters who taught at our local Catholic school. I would walk around at home with a blanket on my head, pretending it was a veil. My father had a difficult time seeing his eldest son like this, and I have a vague recollection of him saying something to my mother about boys not being allowed to behave like this. This was my first lesson in the authoritarian and all-encompassing logic of heterosexism. Later, there were home-staged Christmas pageants where I would occasionally play the part of the Virgin, veiled, again to paternal discomfort. My mother, more subtle in her ways, did not seem to bother about such rigid gender distinctions based on attire. Though I never had the compulsion to dress up in her clothes, I did like touching them, and I still have vivid memories of what some of her dresses looked and felt like.

Later, as I began thinking more and more about entering the seminary to become a priest, I would play at dressing up for mass, with old-fashioned Roman vestments that I sometimes made from recycled sheets. I would occasionally draw different costumes for the religious order that I wanted to found later in life. As an altar boy, I enjoyed the feel of the cassock on me, and I especially liked the red one worn for special feasts. When I became a novice and, after an unassuming robing ceremony, began wearing the simple black cassock of my community, I became a member of a class apart, whose religious dress was the outwardly visible sign of his special election. Shortly after, I gave up on wearing the cassock because I, as well as many others, came to see it as too symbolically charged and constraining in the liberalizing climate engendered by the Second Vatican Council. I retained my fascination, however, with religious uniforms and accoutrements of one sort or another. The garb of the Blessed Sacrament Fathers I considered boring in the extreme: the classic black cassock, sash, and a cloth monstrance worn discreetly over the heart. I liked the black-and-white medieval costume of the Dominicans, and the red-and-black crusader look of the Passionists. There was something gloriously majestic and slightly campy about these outfits. The members of these religious orders became larger than life simply by wearing such outlandish ensembles.

The rich chocolate brown of the Franciscan costume also fascinated me. With its cowl, rope, and rosary, and the occasional sandals, it carried the attractively mysterious aura of simple poverty and harsh missionary work in exotically distant lands. For a brief time, I even thought of becoming a Franciscan monk simply because of what they wore, like Friar Tuck in the *Robin Hood* television series of my youth. Maybe I could have equally exciting adventures in the forest with my own band of handsome merry men! I was therefore quite struck when I first came across the popular pornographic images of the seventeenth and eighteenth centuries showing tumescent monks, usually Franciscan, engaged in a variety of erotic acts with members of either sex, as can sometimes be found in certain editions of the Marquis de Sade's works. Aware of their deeper cultural significance as typical forms of rabid anticlerical and antireligious discourse, I nonetheless found such representations incredibly exciting, combining, as they did, elements of the sacred and the superbly and basely profane. The image of a young erect monk, his habit wide open, touches upon a buried fantasy of mine: that of the handsome holy man ravishing me, caught as he is in the throes of a desperate, hungry passion. My fantasy runs even deeper. No doubt at some time, somewhere, the chaste sons of Francis of Assisi did engage in such abominably beautiful acts of brotherly solicitude. No doubt the memory of their names was erased from the pages of history, or perhaps they simply grew old together in tenderness and anonymity. Much like all those others who ceased to exist because of their delicate, caring vices, vices that heal as much as they are meant to infiltrate and subvert.

A gay fascination with uniforms, whether fueled by a secret attraction to secular or religious power, is nothing unusual, perhaps even something stereotypical. It is the external trappings of manly authority that lead to the inner treasure, the military bearing that leads invariably to the erect phallus, the richly ornamented chasuble to the desirable seminaked savior on the cross. If the chosen uniform has the deceptive simplicity of a Franciscan habit, meant to be worn by poor men in service to the poor, then it becomes charged erotically with the altruism of its wearer. The compelling questions: What is worn underneath, close to the skin, to carry, comfort, and sustain the vital center of such an attractive and powerfully sacred body? What can I do to find out? How can I seduce this holy man? What will it take to find myself under his habit, touching him savagely? How can I make him — and by extension, his fiery god — mine?

In Franco Zeffirelli's stunning film about Francis of Assisi, *Brother Sun, Sister Moon,* the opening sequence depicts the return of Francis from a local war, showing him in bed with a high fever. Presumably, he is near death, and this experience will leave him a profoundly changed man, one whose values and very purpose for existing are no longer those of his father or his culture. The actor who plays the saint is beautiful. Francis lies in bed, wearing a delicate, vaporlike garment. Though not meant to be sexy, the scene manages to convey a strong erotic energy. You want to reach into the screen to wipe his feverish brow, and plant a delicate kiss on his parched lips. You know you are touching a saint, but you still desire him. Despite the sickness, you want to crawl next to him, hold him in your arms, arouse him, let him fall asleep on your shoulder. Later, the film re-creates the famous scene in the town square of Assisi where a naked Francis gives back to his father the clothes he is wearing, and then walks outside the gates toward the calling that awaits him. The cinematographic body of the saint is ravishing. From the back, you admire his shapely buttocks. You know this is all an invention. But you find yourself falling irrationally for the mad, comely saint of Assisi.

When I saw the torn habit and undergarments of Francis in the Assisi basilica, I wanted to kiss them passionately, adore them, wear them next to my burning skin.

Blessed Francis of Assisi, saint of saints, wonder of God's creation, divine rebel, teach us to be more like you. You changed your times. You made possible a new way of seeing and belonging in the world. As a community, help us to understand our own path and our own vision. Guide us. Sustain us. Comfort and reassure us. Instill in us a deep respect for the unique gifts of the earth, as we acknowledge and celebrate their goodness. Help each of us discover his own way, as difficult, cumbersome, or fearsome as it may seem. We ask for your blessings on our endeavors, and we give thanks for your holy and timeless example. Amen.

EIGHT

Dominic Savio
and Other Boy Saints

ETWEEN THE AGES of nine and thirteen, until the time I entered
minor seminary, I was in love with an Italian boy-saint known as
Dominic Savio. For Catholic men of my generation, his story may
be a familiar one. Dominic was born in 1842 to a poor peasant family in the Turin region of northern Italy. He is best known as a pupil
of Saint John Bosco, the great nineteenth-century Italian apostle of
education and social action, who also wrote a pious biography about
him. Dominic Savio lived only a short fifteen years, dying in 1857
from tuberculosis. He was canonized in 1954. As a model of sanctity, he was held up as a shining example of bodily purity, especially
for adolescent boys. It is said that he never committed a single impure sin, either in thought or in deed. His motto was "Death but not
sin," certainly a very drastic code of honor for any teenager. Saint
Dominic Savio's life was actually quite uneventful. It was full of acts
of obedience and little sacrifices and devotions, particularly to the
Virgin Mary. His most dramatic gesture was to prevent a stone fight
between two boys by interposing himself between them with an upraised crucifix. I have a faint recollection of having tried something
similar in the yard of my grammar school. I suspect I was laughed at
quite roundly. Stories of Dominic Savio portray him as someone who
was always wearily cheerful, a trait which, if true, I find somewhat
silly and odious, cynic that I am.

I got to know Saint Dominic Savio because I attended an all-boys
school run by the religious order that Don Bosco founded, the Salesians, whose special purpose was the education of poor, working-class
boys. The Salesians propagated a cult to him, mainly as a way of in-
culcating the boys under their care with certain so-called Christian
values, but also as a means, no doubt, of controlling and channeling
the emerging anarchism of their raging hormones. I really do believe
that I was in love with Dominic Savio. He was my special friend,
my companion, my model. My devotion to him (he was, after all, a
saint) looked very much like that of a lover for his beloved. I recall
asking my mother for a statue of him on one of my birthdays. It was
beautiful. He stood tall and proud, his arm raised up in the legendary
gesture of the peacemaker, holding the crucifix. His clothes were that
of the proper Italian boy of that time, a suit in shades of brown and
green. On his feast day, March 9, I would light a votive candle in front
of the statue and celebrate the day as though it were his birthday. I
prayed to him, probably talked with him, kept images of him, and
even drew his picture in my wide-eyed admiration of him. The most
perfect manifestation of my love and devotion for Dominic was the
vow of purity I took at age eleven or so, in imitation of him. I don't
recall how long it lasted (I was, after all, almost a teenager), but I
remain very grateful for the wisdom of my confessor who saw my
youthful enthusiasm for what it was: the overly dramatic gesture of
an overly pious and immature, though well-intentioned, boy.

Dominic Savio and I had two important things in common. We
both wanted to be priests, and we both wanted to be saints. He never
achieved the former, though he rather splendidly attained the latter. I went part of the way in the former, and, as for the latter, only
time will tell, though I am certainly not holding my breath. There
was something else that I sensed about us, something unspoken yet
deeply attractive. We were different from our young companions,

125

more lonely, less rowdy, more focused on things ethereal and heavenly. In fact, we were both sissies, queer boys, and I suspect that each, in his own time and place, knew it in his innermost heart, as did those around us. Perhaps that is why I thought we were so much in love with each other.

Dominic Savio's face is one of the few saints' faces that I can vividly recall at will. Holy cards show him as very young, actually probably not more than nine or ten, though he was fifteen when he died. He has the classic look of the androgyne: a slightly feminine, angelic face, long eyebrows, bright eyes, perfect features. His hair is longish, but not enough to look like a girl's, and it rests ever so gently on his forehead. As would normally be the case for artists' portraits of saints, he looks frail and pious, unearthly in his stare, as though he had already attained his heavenly reward. He looks perfect. This is, in fact, a type of boyish face that has always attracted me to some men. In my youth, I felt no doubt smitten by this ethereal look of saintly beauty. Though I do not recall if I did, I may have had some deep, unexplainable urge to deposit a chaste kiss on those pouting, sensuous lips. They were ripe for the picking.

I reread Don Bosco's life of Dominic Savio recently. As an adult, one naturally picks up on things that one never really understood as a child. One of the episodes in his life concerns a swimming hole. This is how Don Bosco relates it. "On his way to and from school Dominic ran into a grave spiritual danger from his companions. In the summer heat many youngsters like to bathe in pools, brooks, and ponds. A group of boys, swimming in the nude, often in open places, can face serious bodily dangers, and we have often had to mourn the drowning of several boys and adults. But the spiritual dangers are more serious. How many youngsters mourn the loss of their innocence and attribute the reason to having gone bathing with such lads in those unfortunate places?" Dominic, consistent with his saintly ways, steadfastly resists, and Don Bosco concludes with a sigh

126

of relief: "Thus Dominic...avoided a serious danger which might have resulted in the loss of his priceless innocence and, with that, in countless other sorry consequences."[37] Don Bosco is unfortunately silent on the precise manner in which the young saint could have lost his "priceless innocence," though the tantalizing possibilities are certainly suggestive.

Obviously, something else is happening in this text. Is it possible that our chaste little Dominic Savio may have had impure thoughts for other boys' bodies, that he was actually a bit of a queer boy? If so, then I like him even more now than I did as a child, because I know exactly how he may have felt. When I reread this passage, it was quite a revelation to me. I only wish I could remember how I had perceived it as a twelve-year-old struggling with his own sexual urges. I probably perceived it the same way subconsciously, which may help explain why I had such a thing for Dominic. It may also help explain why, in my innermost heart, I knew full well that I could never be as chaste as my young hero. I would certainly have lost the priceless innocence so much revered by Don Bosco.

I can conjure up lovely images of what could have happened to Dominic in that swimming hole and among those jagged rocks: images of young, muscular bodies and of the sexual games adolescent boys sometimes play, especially with their younger peers. Images of smooth bodies in perpetual motion, running, and grabbing, and caressing, and stroking ever so intensely. Sighs and screams of wonderful release. I can see Dominic suddenly discovering that he likes all this, that he belongs here, that this is the place and the time for him, that this is his path to sanctity, his country of desire. I can see a young saint suddenly understanding that the disciplined erotic life is actually another path to the holy, that homoerotic desire can transform and sharpen your spiritual outlook, making it more inhabited, more incarnated. The Saint Dominic Savio whom Don Bosco wanted us to know is perhaps not the same young saint who wanted to go swimming naked that day.

No doubt, my innocent love story with Saint Dominic Savio is a tale of desire and devotion, of an obsession at once holy and prosaic. It speaks quite eloquently, I believe, of the conflation of a nascent sexuality and a religious fixation, and how the two really nourished and sustained each other. It also gave me an abiding sense of the ever-shifting boundaries between holiness and desire, between the spiritual and the erotic. This was an important life lesson for me. I do not, however, wish to denigrate or reject the validity of my religious devotion to the saint. I think it was genuine. Yet underneath such pious sentiments, reinforcing and challenging them, some other powerful force was at play. I was beginning to sense, ever so uncertainly and acutely, my urges for the company and the bodies of others like me, and that, yes, I could actually fall in love with boys. I was learning same-sex desire, all in the guise of this mad, irrational crush I had on a cute nineteenth-century Italian boy-saint named Dominic Savio.

My obsession with Saint Dominic Savio was very much tied up with my obsession with masturbation. In many ways, this is how the Catholic Church of that time wanted it to be. Dominic was a model for young Catholic boys, not so much because he may have been pious and obedient, but rather because he was pure. Strangely enough, the actual meaning of this purity was never actually spelled out or spoken, though you guessed that Dominic was pure because he never played with himself. Though it may have been hard to imagine this young saint with a real penis (in the Catholic imagination, saints never seem to have genitals), and I'm not sure I ever dared myself to, you instinctively knew that he never allowed himself to indulge in the lonely and exciting, though always guilt-ridden, vice that was self-abuse. The old-fashioned name itself is revealing. It makes you

128

think of excessive flagellation or some obscure sadomasochistic ritual or discipline. It is also a funny term to describe something so intimate — abusing yourself — as though you were hurting yourself in some physical way, or that you were punishing some bad, disobedient child. That, of course, is exactly how the church wanted us to think about it.

Masturbation was the bogeyman of my adolescence. It was *the* sin, the one impure act that I never seemed to rid myself of. My obsession and guilt with it were so extreme that I actually developed a phobia about it. During my novitiate, the novice master sent me for psychiatric consultation precisely because he thought I was caught up in some unhealthy cycle of masturbatory guilt. A good friend of mine told me recently that he felt so guilty when he masturbated that he would recite his act of contrition right after the deed was done, in case he died with such a terrible stain on his soul. As boys, we were always confessing our sins of masturbation, three, four, five times a week. We were constantly being reminded, often in very subtle ways, that it was bad in the eyes of God, that we were less "manly" because of it. In minor seminary, I recall reading a book written by a military chaplain that used images of horses to talk about masturbation. On the one hand, there was the stallion: free, aggressive, masculine, full of vital energy. The implication was that, if you didn't fall prey to the bad habit of masturbation, you would be like a stallion, a strong, proud, defiant male, presumably the better to spread your seed at will by impregnating submissive females. On the other hand, there stood the beast of labor, the castrated horse plowing the fields. The message here was that, if you lost your seed by masturbating, you would lose your energy and become a submissive male, good only for serving others in a subservient role, not a real man's man. I was struck by this way of thinking, and recall reading the book over and over again. I did not want to be a plow horse. I wanted to be a stallion. This chaplain's simplistic understanding had much in common with the rather naive and totally unscientific view, then prevalent in some medical circles, of masturbation as an illness.[38] We used to joke about hairy palms and loss of hair. The problem is that the church still believed in the myths, and that it wanted us to feel intensely guilty about what was, in fact, nothing more than an innocent adolescent rite of passage. In my case, the church succeeded admirably well.

Dominic Savio was my talisman against masturbation. He was strong where I was weak, pure where I was sinful, controlled where I was not. In my innermost self, I no doubt would have preferred playing with his penis, but I knew that he had overcome its desperate cravings, that his penis had been, in some bizarre way, glorified and sanctified. I probably liked mine a bit too much to allow anything like that to happen to it, but I still magically thought that Dominic's protected penis could save mine, that it could pull me away from the mire that were my recurring moments of self-abuse. The problem is that, as guilty as I may have felt, I enjoyed those times. Once, I was masturbating alone in a stall at the seminary. It was the middle of the day. Everyone else was in class. I heard one of the brothers approaching, and then linger. He knew what I was doing. He no doubt enjoyed hearing the familiar noises. I got extremely turned on by this simple fact. Though nothing else happened, it is one of the most intense of my seminary memories.

My love affair with, and devotion to, Saint Dominic Savio taught me about desire, about its inner logic of want and need, and also about its commonly unrequited nature. In similar ways, this was the cycle of masturbation: I desired; I submitted; I found myself alone. More often than not, quite naturally, the objects of my desire and fantasies were the bodies of my friends and classmates, occasionally those of the priests and brothers, and sometimes that of family members. I moved and functioned in a male world where I felt intensely happy and alive, sometimes sexy and desirable, and generally comfortable and secure. I felt much the same way about my Catholic faith and the rituals that I so willingly embraced. I was surrounded, gratefully, by male bodies, whether on the cross or in the black cassock. And if I felt alone, I could turn to the ever present, ever constant saint, my celestial boyfriend, Dominic Savio. He, without a doubt, would fill the empty, gnawing hole. Men, in far more profane ways, still do that to me.

The Salesian school I attended coincidentally brought together the major elements for a homosexual education. First, there was the perfect, intensely desirable Dominic Savio, the boy I could love in the guise of devotion to a saint. He was our standard of behavior, our heroic model. It was through him that I was taught how erotically charged religion — and the Catholic faith in particular — could be. Second, it was during this time in school that I had my first really close friendship with another boy. Christopher was bright and attractive, slightly older, with a freckled face. I always wanted to be with him. I suspect I was in love with him. He would often take care of me if some of the other kids picked on me. Third, there were two teachers who were instrumental in defining complementary types of masculinity for me. My fifth grade teacher was always impeccably dressed, slightly effeminate, well-mannered, but tough with the ruler. I am sure he was gay. Deep down, I knew that he and I were alike, and that is no doubt why I liked him. My sixth grade teacher, excellent pedagogue, was a rugged, intense man, and wonderfully sexy in a fatherly, chain-smoking sort of way. I had a bit of a crush on him. Both these teachers, by simply being who they were, taught me how elastic masculinity could be, and how conditional desire truly was. This Salesian school, dominated by the alluringly sexy Dominic, constituted a unique vortex and site of homosexual affirmation.

I was learning something else about desire, but, in this case, it had to do with its darker, though far more attractive, because more dangerous, side. Saint Dominic Savio had a female counterpart, Saint

Maria Goretti. Like Dominic's, her story is simple, but more dramatic because of the method of her death. A very poor Italian girl, she was only twelve when she was stabbed repeatedly for refusing to submit to the sexual advances of a nineteen-year-old farmhand named Alessandro. Before dying from her wounds, she forgave her murderer. She was canonized in 1950, four years before Dominic Savio. Alessandro was present at the ceremony. Maria Goretti became the Catholic model for young girls, who were encouraged to be like her, even to the point of death, in defending their bodily purity. She was the first female martyr to be canonized, not for having died for the faith, but because she fought for her virginity.

When I was a child, I had a life of Saint Maria Goretti which I read continuously. Maria herself did not interest me, though I certainly respected her sanctity, and I do recall feeling quite upset by what happened to her. The swarthy nineteen-year-old Alessandro, however, as might perhaps be expected, certainly fascinated me. I remember that the story, as with much of the hagiographic literature dealing with martyrs, was written like soft-core pornography, describing the hot Italian midday sun and the sweaty farmhand in grand, glorious detail. The book's atmosphere was intensely charged sexually. I recall one scene in particular. It depicted the entry of the bare-chested Alessandro into the cool peasant house, where Maria was working alone in the kitchen. His so-called "animal" cravings, which were a real turn-on for me, dominated the pages, as he moved ever closer to the source of his sexual need. Though I was only eleven or twelve at the time, I sensed instinctively, even if not quite sure why, that I certainly wanted to submit to him. This feeling excited me intensely. I felt "caught," however, between desire for Alessandro and revulsion for the act he was on the verge of accomplishing. In a strange way, I was able to abstract my sense of the murder about to be committed from the lusty gestures of the aroused semiclad farm laborer. In responding to these erotic signals, I experienced an extraordinary comfort and a sense of inner tranquility. I knew what I wanted, without really knowing who I was. This was a significant beginning in my education of desire. An important element in this very "Catholic" education was no doubt the unconscious association of unsatisfied and frustrated sexual need with the emergence of sanctity: the virgin, martyred or not, as the saving grace, as the sacrificial motif.

Desire naturally knows no boundaries, especially for a gay youngster entering adolescence. My reaction was not against Maria's person or her sanctity, but rather for the erotic needs that the farmhand touched in me, and that he embodied. He was the handsome James Dean to my virginal Dominic Savio, the schoolyard bully to my saintly, though perhaps a bit too pure, heavenly friend. In this case, it was the darkly masculine, vitally necessary, and perversely attractive side of sanctity that fed my emerging desires. These nascent desires were unspoken, if very keenly felt. I had no way of actualizing them, except for what my juvenile imagination might allow me by way of escape. My engagement with Saint Maria Goretti, the young virgin martyr, was therefore an erotic encounter with her killer. It was, in itself, an escape. It spoke to me of rough and hungry men, of dangerous erotic cravings, of desires left unexpressed and unpleased. This dark side was wonderfully attractive. It carried its own spell. How different from Dominic Savio the demanding Alessandro was, and how much I wanted to satisfy him! And how I envied Maria, in a perverse way, for being the object of his burning lust!

In the annals of Catholic sainthood, child saints tend to be found mostly in the categories of the early martyrs. In fact, most of them are anonymous. The most juvenile are the Holy Innocents, male newborns who were killed on the orders of Herod when the Magi, traveling to find the infant Jesus, revealed that they were seeking the new king of Israel. The church has canonized young saints, mostly adolescent, but they are few and far between. In itself, this is a strange phenomenon. Normally, such saints have lived out their short lives in relative obscurity, but have attained unusual heights of excessive piety or mortification. Most are members of major religious orders, who have advocated quite strenuously for their canonization. These saints become models for youth, even though their peculiar paths to sanctity do not really reflect the everyday concerns and lifestyles of ordinary adolescents. The church imposes models of sanctity for young people, partly for reasons of moral (often sexual) convenience, but also because she wishes to inculcate a sense of the possibility of a religious vocation.

Maria Goretti and Dominic Savio were, by far, the most universally accessible of the saintly models for youth. Interestingly enough, they were also ordinary laypersons. This made them especially attractive and effective as examples. For boys of my era, however, other saints were occasionally invoked. Among these, there was a trio of young Jesuits: Saint Stanislaus Kostka (1550–68), Saint Aloysius Gonzaga (1568–91), and Saint John Berchmans (1599–1621). Aloysius Gonzaga is the patron of youth; John Berchmans, of altar boys. Dominic Savio is actually the patron of children and teenagers. There was a fourth saint, less popular for youth, but much better known and revered as the patron of expectant mothers: a Redemptorist lay brother, Saint Gerard Majella (1726–55). It is worth noting that this Jesuit triumvirate (respectively of Polish, Italian, and Belgian descent) was very much tied to the expansionist origins of the Jesuits as a religious order, and to their wish to attract vocations by creating saintly models for incoming novices to emulate. Of them all, Saint Aloysius Gonzaga was the best known, mainly because of the fact that he rejected the family fame and wealth to which he was born, but also because, until the arrival of Dominic Savio, he embodied the perfect model of boyish chastity and purity, as did Stanislaus Kostka, with whom he was often paired.

Religious orders were, and remain, the great producers of saints. The Salesians had Dominic Savio; the Jesuits, their young trio; and

the Redemptorists, Gerard Majella. The Franciscans and Dominicans, the other two major orders, no doubt had their own young
saints. Which boy saint you knew or were taught to imitate very
much depended on which religious congregation happened to be a
part of your life, either in your parish church or at school. In my
case, the religious order to which I would later belong, the Congregation of the Blessed Sacrament, being relatively young, had no other
saint than its founder, Peter Julian Eymard. It therefore adopted its
own young saint, Saint Tarcisius, primarily because of his association with the Eucharist. This need that male religious orders had to
possess within their ranks exemplars of youthful sanctity was a ped-
agogical one. Particularly in their seminary formation, they wanted
to use boy saints as models of the behavior appropriate to the order's
given mission. These boy saints became icons of what the perfect
religious-in-formation should strive to reflect and embody in their
daily lives. Of all the Christian virtues appropriate to this station,
chastity was, by far, the most important. Boy saints were nothing if
not castrated boys. Boy saints never masturbated. One was not even
sure if they had a real penis.

The Jesuits, their saints and their training, occupied a special niche
in my life. I was never a member of the order (though I applied, and
was refused, after leaving my own). But within the Catholic imagination, Jesuits stand, by far, as the most privileged and attractive
of all the male religious congregations. Jesuits have always hovered
about me: through their colleges (Holy Cross, and Loyola College
of Montreal); through their manly, engaging saints (Ignatius of Loyola, Francis Xavier, the North American martyrs); through their
heroic members (Daniel Berrigan, most notably); and through the
spiritual direction provided by former and current Jesuit friends and
colleagues. When I was completing my postulancy at the provincial
house of my order in New York City in the summer of 1970, a colleague and I would sometimes hang out with a Jesuit novice living

not far from us. I think I had a crush on him. Actually, I suspect we both did, as did he. The Jesuits sporadically have been sources of desire for me. I never developed a pious devotion for Aloysius Gonzaga or Stanislaus Kostka, primarily because I was not really familiar with them, but I have been known to hanker after the occasional flesh-and-blood Jesuit. Whether or not they were saintly is another question. Perhaps I was hoping not.

By his very existence, the boy-saint, particularly the virginal boy-saint, poses a problem. In communities of celibate, older men, what exactly can be his role and place? In his other-worldly persona, does he represent innocence sublimated, or rather innocence awaiting corruption? Does the image of the boy-saint play upon the theme of pedophilia, subsume it, make it symbolically possible and viable? As an object of veneration, is he the community plaything, while also serving as the saintly incarnation of the community values and divine purpose? Boy-saints are unreal boys for forbidden desires. They can absorb, within their holiness, all the erotic fantasies and needs of men who would want nothing better than to possess them and corrupt them, but who know that this should not be done with real boys. Boy-saints, in their holy innocence, deflect material desire.

My love for Saint Dominic Savio was innocent to the point of naïveté. I wish I could remember, some forty years later, how I might really have felt, and how I might have expressed it, if at all, but it escapes me. Did I ever respond to him sexually? As a youngster, did I ever masturbate while fantasizing about him? Did I ever long for him to touch me in some dark, forbidden place? Did I ever actually play out with others my sentimental crush on the saint? Where did my sweet devotion to Dominic Savio end and my infatuation with other boys begin? Or were they one and the same? Now, at fifty, perhaps I can allow myself a time of fantasy, a passing moment of escape into youthful desire. Perhaps I can re-create my time of love.

In my imagination, I go back to the age of twelve. In my room, which I like to keep very orderly, I have converted my bureau into an altar. I have several statues on it. In a place of honor stands that of Dominic Savio. It is a mild spring Sunday. I am alone. Having just come back home from serving early morning mass, I am changing my clothes. I look at the statue of my favorite saint. He is smiling at me, with a look of beatitude on his face. I know that he is beckoning me. I kneel in front of the altar, naked. I pray: "Please, Saint Dominic Savio, tell me what I should do. Today at mass, Philip, the other altar boy, told me that he wanted to be my friend. I like Philip. He reminds me of you. I touched his hand. It was wonderful. Will you touch my hand? Can I be Philip's friend, just like you are my friend? Can I kiss Philip, like I sometimes kiss your statue? Oh, Saint Dominic Savio, help me to know why I feel this way." And he answers: "I love you, Donald. You are my special friend. I like it when we play together, when you touch yourself and think about me. Philip is a nice boy. He likes you too, just as I do. I want you to be with me, Donald. When you play with Philip, I will be there with you. Think of me. Think of the three of us together. Don't worry, Donald. You can kiss Philip, just like you sometimes kiss me." I look down at myself, an erection in hand. If I were that boy — as I wish I had been — my joy would have been boundless. None of this, of course, ever happened, much as I might dream about it. Regrettably, Dominic always stayed on his distant pedestal. I never knew Philip. But, as with much else in childhood, the line often blurs between fact and fiction. My knowing and loving Saint Dominic Savio is what allowed me, much later, to know, want, and indeed love all the "Philips" of my gay life.

I never really wanted to be as chaste as my young hero, Dominic Savio. If anything, I wanted him to feel within himself the painful and urgent cravings of my spent force.

Blessed Dominic Savio, beloved of my youth, saint most seductive, I beseech your blessings on me. You were my lesson in desire, my boyish fixation. Your life was one of simple gestures of grace. Teach me to see the glory of the divine in the everyday. Your purity was a model and a comfort for me. Teach me how to remain in your virtuous shadow. Above all, protect and shepherd our gay youth. Help them come to a realization and acceptance of themselves as children of the divine. Support their awkward steps; guide their fragile hearts. Be their sweet refuge in times of fear. Shower us all with your youthful goodness. Amen.

NINE

Damien and the Missionary Saints

M ISSIONARIES HAVE ALWAYS fascinated me. Even from an early age, I admired the exoticism of their lives, and the altruism that seemed to motivate them. Everything about them struck me as different and exciting. They traveled to distant lands, had thrilling, never-ending adventures, met unusual people, and they did it all for a good and noble cause. No doubt some of my idealism and enthusiasm stemmed from the natural urges of a young boy for the sheer fun of it all. Another part of me, however, was quite serious about the religious dimension of the missionary enterprise, and the commitment and hard work it necessitated. I thought I might want to be a missionary when I grew up. I was a bit naive, thinking sentimentally that I could fearlessly spread the Christian message *and* have a good time doing it, even under the most difficult and strenuous of circumstances. That, of course, may have motivated me even further. My youthful imagination craved unfamiliar and out-of-the-ordinary experiences, preferably in distant lands, the better, I would guess, to resign myself to inhabiting the environment in which I had been born.

Times have naturally changed, and we have become far more realistic and critical about the colonial and imperial aspects of the missionary effort. History has sadly witnessed the severe cultural and sometimes health ravages caused by the good, though misplaced, intentions of missionaries. We no longer accept the so-called civilizing work carried out by these men and women, conscious that it very often hides sinister political or economic ends. Missionary work does not carry the luster and exotic appeal it once did. We tend to equate it with proselytizing of the most odious and duplicitous sort, a kind of universal "McDonaldization" of different cultures, an empty and futile attempt to re-create the world in our own Christian image.

The religious culture in which I grew up as a child was a missionary one. In the last century, the province of Quebec, per capita, sent out more nuns, brothers, and priests to the foreign mission fields than any other part of the Roman Catholic world. This was coupled with a prodigious number of foundations of missionary religious orders, several of which tended to be quite specialized in their field or country of activity. Two factors can help explain this phenomenon. First, there was a surplus of religious personnel in the province. Vocations stood at an all-time high, and mission work was a convenient and attractive way to dispose of excess labor. Second, and perhaps more significantly, the church in Quebec saw itself very much as a missionary church, in large part because it also perceived itself as being more orthodox and pristine in its appropriation of Roman teaching. It was therefore a "cleaner" Catholicism, more exportable, and, by extension, more desirable in terms of its religious message of conversion. This proprietary sense of missionary work necessarily fixed the relatively high esteem in which missionaries were held in Quebec, thereby coloring, if only by ricochet, my own vocational designs.

Oddly enough, I did not choose a missionary order when it finally came time to enter seminary, but a more sedentary, parish-based one. I do not really remember why. For a time, I flirted briefly with the idea of joining a group known as the Oblates of Mary Immaculate (OMI), whose extensive missionary work in the Canadian West was highly regarded, though less so now because of the issue of abuse in native residential schools. The other order that intrigued me greatly was the White Fathers, so named because of their totally white garb, whose exclusive sphere of missionary activity was the African continent. But Africa frightened me slightly, and it was far too exotic a locale. I had not known any black person to that point in my life, and the idea of spending a good chunk of my life south of the equator did not appeal to me. I was also ignorant. My only images of Africa, apart from the standard *National Geographic* pictures of bare-breasted women, were of Tarzan, who had far more to do with my confused libido than with anything truly or remotely real or insightful about Africa itself. Mine was a limited world.

For several years as a boy, there was a popular television show, hosted by a White Father, that I relished. Known as Père (Father) Ambroise, and strikingly handsome in a professorial sort of way, he was a wonderful communicator. I think the weekly show was telecast on Sundays. He had done extensive missionary work, had traveled a fair amount, and his talks were always full of significant cultural insights and high tales of adventure. Well before it was intellectually fashionable, he would carefully explain, often with the help of pictures and artifacts, the myths, legends, and stories of a given culture, and do so with sensitivity and respect. I liked him. He was learned (or so he appeared to my young eyes), spoke eloquently, and certainly seemed to live an exciting life, even if he was only a missionary (or perhaps because of it). His weekly television shows were my first real exposure to the far broader universe of cultural difference and variety beyond my narrow confines of family and school. He imparted to me a desire for knowledge, for travel, for stories, and for the richness of cultures. The fact that I may have found him attractive in some way only added to his charm. He was seductive as only good teachers can and should be, and I allowed myself to be engrossed by his television charisma. In reflecting back, I can see that he was teaching me how to look across, and through, my small world to the bigger one beckoning. I call this the anthropology of desire, and in subtle ways I now understand why only a missionary could seduce me in this delightfully fiendish way. He was the right missionary at the right time and place. I was ready for my conversion. I do not know if Père Ambroise is a saint, or even on his way to becoming one, but I am confident that his positive and beneficial influence on countless other young people from my generation should qualify him for some special consideration. He opened our souls to the world, when so much conspired to keep them hermetically shut.

The anthropology of desire was not limited to real missionaries talking about real cultures, however exotic and remote from my own. It could also be imagined, and one of the most significant and lasting sources of my early education in same-sex desire was a self-reliant fictional character stranded alone on a distant island. He may not have been a missionary in the religious sense of the term, but he epitomized for me the determination and force of character that I readily associated with the generous propagators of the faith. This character was, of course, Robinson Crusoe, from the novel by Daniel Defoe. He was the hero of a book that I read continuously at the age of eleven or twelve. Several aspects of his story appealed to me. The first had to do with his enforced solitude. I was a bit of a loner, so I resonated to the simple pleasures he took from having to carve out a place for himself in an alien world, and to impose order and coherence upon it. Though no doubt difficult, this struck me as a worthy and noble task, one born of contingency as much as innate gratification. A second motif centered on the locale for the story: this unknown, deserted island, an Eden in miniature, awaiting some human intervention for something momentous to happen. I liked this idea of starting from scratch, of a man's actions creating new beginnings and new promises, of utopia finally met and fulfilled.

But without a doubt, the most engaging and delicious part of the story was how two men, Robinson and his man Friday, could construct a world together: two lost men, alone, needing each other to survive, perhaps falling in love, certainly having loud sex on the empty beach. My young queer heart had never known such sweet palpitations! What scenarios I would invent in my enflamed mind! Friday was all mystery and exotic charm, while Robinson was the rational, civilized one. My unformed mind did not grasp the all too heavy subtext of colonialism at work here. Rather, I remained quite fascinated by the rapport between the two men, awkward and stilted at first, but fast transformed into one of mutual care and affection. Such steamy scenarios I devised: naked torsos, sweaty and muscular, straining under the hot sun; a sensual bath in the cold sea, fingers at attention; a shared meal, lovingly prepared; hot sex and cuddles under the moonlight; a gentle sleep. This was the very first time that I had come across a story where two men making a life together for themselves seemed like a real possibility, even though it may have been by force of circumstance. Regardless, it made me happy, proud, and jealous. Somewhere deep inside me, I knew I wanted the same thing, and hope kept me confidently coming back to these inspiring and uplifting pages by Defoe.

Tarzan, another fictional character, also taught me much about desire. I never really knew him in his comic book incarnation, but I do recall one or two films that particularly struck my fancy. Again, the text was all about racial (and racist) distinctions, and a helpless blond woman and an idealistic though naive missionary were invariably involved as part of the skimpy plot, as were the usual assortment of stunned and innocent natives. Tarzan stands out as one of the few heroic figures from my childhood, perhaps more by virtue of what he did not wear than because of any especially stunning feats of manly daring. His wonderfully all-but-naked body raised all sorts of troublesome questions in my mind, most having to do with semiclothed, strangely secretive body parts. He was quite different from the practical Robinson Crusoe, more macho and steamy, but each embodied, in his own way, same-sex need and desire. Each, in fact, represented an attractive and complementary form of masculinity; each was able to elicit in me comforting yet disturbing feelings of passion and need. Each touched me in my innermost secret place. And though missionaries were often nowhere to be seen in the stories, the alien allure of the fictional settings guaranteed their surreal, almost religious, appeal for me, as though heaven itself were beckoning.

In minor seminary, we would have a required one-hour period of spiritual reading every Sunday evening, usually after supper, from seven to eight. The apparent intent was to "elevate" our minds at the end of the Lord's Day, presumably to get us thinking about more uplifting matters than sports and the next day's math exam, and also perhaps — God forbid! — the bestial body of the boy sprawling next to us in the study hall. We read what we wanted, though we would sometimes have to advise the school's spiritual director of exactly what it was we had chosen. For this purpose, a collection of inspiring books was kept at the back of the study hall. It consisted mostly of an odd mixture of lives of the saints: odd not because of the biographical part, but rather because of the eclectic saints in question. I remember reading stories about strange individuals — all men, of course — who had spent their lives combating the temptations of alcohol (we were too young to drink), cards (we had no idea what poker was, never mind the stripping part), or impure thoughts (aha!). I would invariably search out the latter. The reading often turned out to be more titillating than spiritually inspiring.

One book that I do recall reading more than once, and always with a great deal of fascination, was the life of a young Belgian missionary who had spent time among the lepers of Hawaii, eventually catching the disease and dying there himself. I had no idea what leprosy was, except that it had to be something gross and disgusting. I had a faint recollection of having seen some lepers in the movie *Ben Hur*, and I knew that Christ had healed some in the gospels. And Hawaii was a very, very exotic place in my untraveled imagination, almost a paradise on earth. It seemed close enough to be familiar (it was, after all, an American state), yet different enough to appear fantastic. The missionary in question was Blessed Damien (Joseph) De Veuster, better known as Damien of Molokai.

The April 15 entry on Damien in *Butler's Lives of the Saints* reads like a typical account of saintly devotion, tribulation, and eventual vindication.[39] Born in 1840 to a modest farming family in Belgium, Damien followed his brother into religious life, replacing him as a missionary to the Hawaiian Islands in 1864. He volunteered to serve at the leper colony on the Island of Molokai, spent almost all of his life there caring for the isolated inhabitants, raising funds for their material needs and for the construction of clinics and schools, and finally dying himself as a leper at the age of forty-nine. In his day, he was considered a controversial figure, within and outside his own religious community, and his somewhat autocratic manner was not always well appreciated. Though he was able to build support for the colony, the medical and social fear of leprosy remained, and Damien found himself the unfortunate victim of both his own success and of a deeply stigmatized and misunderstood disease.

Butler's summary includes the following rather interesting and revealing notation, which raises intriguing issues about the intersections between sanctity and sexuality:

Molokai was called "the Devil's Island" and "the Devil's paradise," because it was believed that its inhabitants lived a dissolute life with no regard for either human or divine laws. While Damien was motivated by a limitless love for his fellow human beings and a spirit of total sacrifice, not everyone (including some of his superiors) understood his motives. He was to be accused of not keeping his vow of obedience in remaining on Molokai, of being too interested in material things because he raised large sums of money to help the lepers, and, most seriously of all, of not keeping his vow of celibacy. This last accusation arose from the belief of the day that leprosy was most commonly transmitted by sexual contact, and so, when Damien eventually contracted the disease, he was accused of having broken his vows. As a result, on the orders of his superiors, he underwent three humiliating medical examinations aimed at establishing his chastity.[40]

I am not sure what those three sessions consisted of, but I can imagine that, given the state of medical knowledge of the day about sexuality, they must have been crude and indeed quite humiliating. How do you establish and confirm a presumably heterosexual man's chastity? I might guess at how you could possibly do it for a gay man, but even that requires some leap of the imagination. Is it possible that Damien was suspected of sodomy, apparently a more easily established medical diagnosis, and that his troublesome anus was the real symbolic issue at stake, not his celibacy?

Such a question raises the broader, and far more intriguing, issue of the sexuality of saints generally, and how their bodies can be transformed into scripts for the projection and cataloguing of certain cultural fears. As cultural products in their own right, in their lives as well as through their cults, saints capture many of the tensions and contradictions of a particular society, and some of the more significant and revealing of these have to do with the "darker" forces of human sexuality. Saints have often been accused of shameful sexual misconduct, of being secretly perverse or physically excessive, or of indulging in obscene vices. While some of this is undoubtedly politically motivated, clearly aimed at undermining the religious, institutional, or theological credibility of a saintly individual, much of it copies the more irrational anxieties and fears associated with certain forms of troublesome sexual desire or behavior. In this process, suspicions or outright accusations of sodomy have stood out as particularly effective strategies (the anus being especially problematic culturally), as might, in our own age, those having to do with pedophilia or child abuse of any sort. Saints are sometimes accused of indulging in these things, not because they have necessarily done so, but rather because they embody a certain pristine incorruptibility. And this, more than any other "perversion," is most unsettling culturally.

Whether or not Damien remained chaste does not really matter, though it may be relevant in establishing his claims to sainthood. What hit me upon reading this passage was how it confirmed Michel Foucault's observations about the deployment of discourses of power — in this case, medical and religious — in the control of sexuality, and how the perceived infringement of sexual normativity can be used, in turn, as a privileged means of undermining moral and spiritual worth and credibility. I suspect Damien's superiors were interested in far more than simply his purity of body; that this was a way finally of asserting the primacy of their collective will over his, and their ultimate control over his successful mission. Through the cold and impersonal hands of the medical specialists, these clerical virtuosi were raping Damien, a kind of religiously inspired gang bang. The other quite interesting dimension to this episode is the way in which a particularly odious degenerative disease, leprosy, was culturally conflated with sexual excess, again a very common historical pattern. This opens up important avenues for further reflection about our own apparently enlightened scientific age, especially in the case of how perceptions around AIDS developed and became culturally inscribed, given that both medical conditions still share similar characteristics in the popular imagination.

There was a cardinal archbishop of Montreal (at one point in the 1960s, he was considered possible papal material) who left his ecclesiastical seat in 1967 to work with lepers in Africa and to concentrate on providing philanthropic aid to needy areas of the Third World. As a young priest, he had dreamed of being a missionary, and he did serve briefly in Japan for a while prior to the war. Considered elitist and autocratic during his pre–Vatican II years as archbishop, he subsequently played a positive and highly visible role in the liberalization of the Catholic Church in Quebec. His was the voice that I heard droning away on the radio as a child when we would be forced to recite the rosary in the evenings in my maternal grandmother's kitchen. Many years later, I met this man in the context of a university honorary degree ceremony. I was his escort for the day. As with Paul VI, this cardinal was known to be a homosexual, and he was always reputed to have had his favorites among the seminary students under his care. When I saw him that day (he was confined to a wheelchair because of his health), he was accompanied by a most attractive and strapping assistant who immediately caught my eye. I understood. Later, I was told by this same individual that His Eminence had particularly appreciated my care and attention, and that he had "felt close to me." No doubt. Oddly enough, I had sensed a similar connection between us. Over lunch, the cardinal, a bit confused in talking about his past, regaled us with stories, some repetitious, about his missionary efforts among the African lepers. He kept giving me knowing looks, bless him. He was still able to do so despite his age, and I indulged him gracefully. But sitting here recounting this story, I wonder if this cardinal, like Damien, had ever been the passive object of the sexual misgivings and suspicions of his superiors. Being a Prince of the Church, probably not. The cardinal's ecclesiastical backside was safe. A stark lesson in clerical power and privilege.

In my seminary reading of Damien's rather romanticized life, however, I do not remember anything coming up about his medical examinations, and thankfully so. I am not sure I could have handled it, though I certainly would have relished trying to figure out all the possible medical permutations and combinations. I preferred my saints to be of a somewhat safer sort, not raising too many unsettling questions, saints like Dominic Savio or the young Tarcisius, on whom I could simply and conveniently project my eager needs and fantasies. Yet Damien did raise some tough issues for me, and, for once, they were not of a sexual nature. I was enamored with him because he seemed so committed, so sure of his place, so totally giving to others. I admired his incredible sense of altruism, and I idolized him intensely because of it. Damien shed a sharply burning light on my vocation, and his example, as extreme as it may have seemed for someone of my age and social condition, nagged at me. Actually, it motivated me, for it made me see, somewhat rather starkly, that everyone has a calling, and that one needs to follow that calling regardless.

For a gay boy, certainty of calling is not, by any stretch of the imagination, a given, something cast in stone from all time. Our lives are far too contingent to allow for such guarantees. We are always struggling to carve out a place and a home for ourselves, a life space that we can rightfully call our own. A sense of vocation is not something given or owed to us; rather, it remains uncertain and fortuitous, though some would argue that it is, at its heart, a gift of grace. This was also the 1960s, the times they were a-changing, the era of civil rights and the Peace Corps, so Damien's radical altruism was quite fashionable. I was certainly motivated, captivated, and inspired by Damien's model of engagement, but I found myself uncertain about my own. Should I also go off and take care of lepers or other social outcasts (unlikely), or should I rather become a good and docile priest (more likely)? Nagging at the back of my mind was the growing awareness, thankfully often hidden in my subconscious, of my

149

attraction to other boys. How could I possibly ever reconcile this with some grand, altruistic life purpose?

This question, I believe, lies at the heart of the gay vocation in the world, and of gay spirituality and sanctity more specifically. It summons us to consider how and why we do what we do, and the reason that our vocation so often lies in areas of beauty, creativity, and service. Much has been written about the fertile manifestations of our marginality. I will put forth a radical proposition, though it is historically impervious to proof. I venture to say that a significant, if not a predominant, number of male saints have been homosexual, that they have struggled with the meaning of same-sex desire in their lives, most often for the person of Christ, that some succumbed to their sexual urges, while others chose quite consciously to sublimate their needs in works of heroic Christian virtue and fortitude. And, furthermore, that such needs and desires, as evil, sinful, or condemnable as they were thought to be by the saints themselves or by any number of "godly" others, have been the core, fundamental forces for good, motivating, sustaining, nourishing, and inspiring these great works.

This is not simply a romantic take on religion as a surrogate for sex, though one should not dismiss the equation too readily. Queering male sanctity, making it a site for unstable discourses of gender and sex, identity and transgression, spirituality and power, implies that we also consider and accept the very real possibility that some of the persons implicated may have actually been queer in their desires. When, as a young seminarian unsure of himself and how he could relate to the desirable bodies of other boys, I sat there quietly reading the life of the heroic Damien, missionary of Molokai, pondering its secret meaning, I was undergoing a queer transformation of my own. I read the subtle signs that Damien's life was throwing at me, and I was beginning to believe that I too could make a difference similar to the one he made. I picked up on the queer Damien, the destroyer of taboos and false medical verities, the lover and partner of outcasts, the sexual victim, and I resonated to the strength and beauty of his vocation. His courage tempered the shape and texture of my own fragile sense of calling.

One other mission figure has fascinated me by the legends of his exceptional life of commitment and hard work, but also by the beautiful portraits one can sometimes see of him: Saint Francis Xavier, the great Jesuit missionary to the Far East. In reading about his travels, one is struck by the close parallels with those of the Apostle Paul. A learned man, and one of Saint Ignatius of Loyola's very first followers, he opened up vistas in India, Malaysia, Indonesia, and Japan. On Malacca, near the place where his relics were first buried after his death, there towers an impressive statue of him on a panoramic hill, an abandoned church bearing his name close by. The spirit of Francis Xavier permeates all of Far Eastern Catholic culture and legend, from the converts of insular colonial Goa to the intercultural incursions of Matteo Ricci in imperial xenophobic China. Xavier is the missionary's missionary (he was named patron of foreign missions), a man of tempered vision, boundless energy, and unwavering religious commitment.

His iconography shows him as a classically dark and handsome Spaniard, young (he was only forty-six when he died), slim, and tall, almost a gay clone from the 1970s. In fact, this is generally the way Jesuit saints and martyrs were artistically portrayed (the North American Martyrs being a prime example), which raises the intriguing question of why this would be so. On closer examination, one notices that each saint bears a rather striking resemblance to Ignatius of Loyola. The presumed objective is to demonstrate a direct line of saintly descent from, and communion with, the spirit and charisma of the founder himself. It also re-creates the idea of a collective of men, manly individuals who do not need "feminized" individuality, but whose virility comes first and foremost from their shared identity. This is homosocial and homoerotic bonding at its most rudimentary level, of men with, for, in, and among other men exclusively. Groupings of male saints, or male saints claiming a common spiritual tradition, tend to be shown in this way. Even the twelve apostles all look like Jesus, and it sometimes becomes difficult to separate one from the other, which simply reinforces the common message of affinity and reciprocity, but also of doctrinal orthodoxy and coherence. Each for one, and one for all.

Francis Xavier and Damien of Molokai share the other familiar trait of missionary saints: their intense and necessary solitude, a price to be paid for the privilege of serving in exotic faraway places. In the case of Damien, the solitude was not only a geographical one, imposed by virtue of physical distance, but also a moral and hygienic one. Leprosy literally set him off from others, in the most basic and dehumanizing way possible. His disease was the most visible mark of his difference and isolation. Even prior to falling victim to its disfiguring ravages, the simple fact that he worked with lepers made him suspiciously contagious, both sexually and morally. Guilt by association. As for Francis Xavier, his solitude stemmed from the sharp and disorienting differences of culture, from the risky and discordant encounter of East and West. Though he certainly endured the hardships of travel and distance, and despite his remarkable success in overcoming them, he remained an outsider, the perennial foreigner alone in his culturally bound landscape.

I obviously did not become a missionary, and perhaps I would have had I paid closer attention to the exotic and enticing promptings of Père Ambroise. Leaving home to become a simple priest was perhaps as much as I could muster by way of an adventure. But there are different ways of becoming a missionary in spirit, if not in fact, and the odyssey I have since followed, particularly my work in the area of gay spirituality, has, I believe, been a type of missionary work of its own. My aim may not be conversion, but neither is it beside the point. I prefer to seduce.

As I reflect on Damien, alone and bereft of support on his leprous island, I think I would have claimed him as mine, an angry way to shut up those insipid superiors of his.

Blessed Damien of Molokai, friend of lepers and outcasts, servant of the dejected, we come to you in humble prayer and supplication, seeking your blessing and your tender mercy. You were courageous and exemplary in your devotion to the most helpless and disenfranchised of all. You gave yourself as a victim to be with them in their isolation and social ostracism. You took care of the sick, fed the hungry, clothed the naked, gave comfort to the afflicted, buried the dead. We pray you, grant that we may possess a small portion of your generous selflessness. You were an active defender of their full rights as human beings. Grant us the grace and determination to follow your example. Bless the lepers of our day, those suffering from the unjust stigma of AIDS. And help us reach out to them, as you did so tenderly and passionately. Amen.

TEN

Peter Julian Eymard
and the Eucharist

A T AGE THIRTEEN, I entered high school seminary with a Roman
Catholic order of priests and brothers known as the Congregation of the Blessed Sacrament. It is a small group, founded in the late
1880s in France by Saint Peter Julian Eymard. Saint Eymard, as we
referred to him, was known as the Apostle of the Eucharist. Canonized during the Second Vatican Council in 1962 by Pope John XXIII,
he had been, during his lifetime, a member of the Society of Mary
(the Marists). He left to found a group of priest-adorers whose entire ministry would be dedicated to the real presence of Christ in the
Eucharist. I stayed with the congregation for five and a half years,
until I was midway through my novitiate at the age of eighteen. I
then left because I was in love with another seminarian, who had
also left some months previously. I call this period of my life "my
school for desire." It was in this exceptional atmosphere, I believe,
that I came to an appreciation of my fascination and sense of comfort
with other males.

As its name will attest, the congregation's special mission and
charisma were to spread devotion to the Eucharist. At the time I
entered in the early 1960s, this took the form of perpetual, 'round-
the-clock adoration of the exposed host. Very regal and kitschy
thrones of adoration were found in each of the order's houses
throughout the world, and the religious would relay themselves night
and day (twice during the day, once at night) in praying before the

monstrance. The kingship of Christ was then the central spiritual motif. In minor seminary (called Eymard Preparatory Seminary), I recall that the throne of exposition had a globe with the monstrance sitting somewhat precariously on top, and a stylized crown overhead. By the time the far-reaching liturgical reforms of the Second Vatican Council rolled around, and I had entered novitiate, this military routine of the changing of the guard in the presence of the divine monarch had given way to the far more amorphous rule of individual "prayer before the Eucharist," when and as one saw fit. The theme of the Eucharist as a meal, the mass, was now predominant.

On the surface of things, I chose this particular religious order because I wanted to be a priest, and they were the ones who happened to staff my parish church. I think I was also attracted to an enticing erotic possibility. Something deeper was at work. I was with a group whose very purpose was the adoration of, and devotion to, the Eucharistic body of Jesus himself, the most perfectly desirable of all males. My closed seminary world was replete with young, beautiful male bodies: in the classrooms, showers, playing fields, and dormitories, but also in my moments of silent prayer before the exposed body of my God in the monstrance. I was being taught to make this divine body and blood the center of my life and spirituality, under the guise of the material species of bread and wine. We were always being told that ours was a very special Eucharistic mission, that we were called to be witnesses to the continuing mystery and presence of the Incarnation, God-made-flesh. The fleshy attributes of my fellow seminarians over which I lingered in my furtive looks were, for me, not that much different from the sacred Eucharistic flesh that I was summoned to worship in my vocation as a Blessed Sacrament religious. I was deeply and irrevocably engaged with desirable male bodies, both divine and far more earthly and earthy ones. The line marking religious devotion from erotic desire was extremely fine. I liked being caught up with the body of Jesus, with his flesh and with his blood. Getting up in the middle of the night to spend an hour in solitary prayer, fatigue aside, or perhaps because of it, can be an intensely sensual affair. Adoring the host all alone at 3:00 a.m., one is bound to harbor unusual and heretical thoughts, if not sexy ones.

Being with other boys on a daily basis, in an atmosphere of heightened religious intensity, taught me much with respect to masculine comradeship. It was in the seminary that I began to understand and, more importantly, like my responses to other males. I very much liked the tingling feelings they aroused in me. I liked the look, smell, and crude playfulness of their awkward yet intensely desirable bodies. I liked their early morning erections in the communal showers, or the sweaty odor of their locker room antics. I liked watching them strut around in their white briefs, or stand naked as they bent over to towel themselves. I liked the creaking of their bedsprings at night as they tried to masturbate ever so quietly. I liked watching the bare-chested upperclassmates shaving themselves in the mirror next to me in the morning. I liked seeing them run and grunt on the playing fields and basketball courts. I really liked it when I was sweetly befriended by them, touched and horseplayed with, as one might with a younger brother. It was in this liking that I was taught the discipline of desire, and in its softly burning yet uncertain intensity that I slowly discovered who and what I was.

Over this adolescent kingdom ruled the black-cassocked sons of Saint Peter Julian Eymard, the founder. His image was everywhere. Severe and angular looking, his bony countenance was meant to be our inspiration and our guide. Like him, we were expected to become model adorers of Jesus in the Eucharist. There was indeed something oddly fascinating about his face, though it might appear quite forbidding to others. My favorite is a bust by the great French sculptor Auguste Rodin. Rodin was one of Eymard's first novices in his fledgling congregation. He sculpted the saint's face in bronze, but Eymard did not like it because he thought it made him look too diabolical. Wisely, however, he told the sculptor that his true vocation was not the contemplative life, but rather that of the artist. Saint Peter Julian's bust is no doubt one of Rodin's youthful works, but it is a sentimental favorite of mine. It is a wild and passionate piece: Eymard's features are sharp and jagged, and his wild hair stands on end as though it were alive with fire. This is an image of a man with a mission. I have a picture of me in profile standing next to the original sculpture in the Rodin Museum in Paris. Though I appear considerably younger than I am now, I strike an earnest and serious pose. I recall sensing the importance of the moment, caught up in the vivid historical and religious symbolism of Rodin and Eymard conversing about the merits of this same piece. Somehow, having followed in the saint's footsteps part of the way, and as one of his prodigal sons, I felt entitled to stand there.

The more traditional iconography of Saint Peter Julian Eymard shows him in profile, a mantle over his shoulders, his clothed hands clutched around a monstrance that he holds upright (sometimes at chest level), and that he gazes at with a beatific countenance. This was the statue that greeted us at the entrance to minor seminary, and it is the same image that was so much a part of my visual world in the parish church where my early vocation was nurtured. I found it to be a comfortable, paternal image. It epitomized both a sense of priestly vocation and one of religious devotion and focus. Much to my delight many, many years later, the gay French artists Pierre et Gilles, in their photographic series on the saints, re-created this exact same image, but with a distinctly homoerotic flavor. A beautiful young man, with similar props, assumes the same pose as Saint Eymard. He gazes intently upward, his eyes sparkling with affection and desire. There was something of a vindication in this carnal image, a merging of my early vocation as a son of Eymard with my latent longings for men, as though the artists had tapped into a secret connection, brilliantly exposing it to the light of day. It was like coming out to myself all over again.

For me, Saint Peter Julian Eymard was the father, the guide, the path to follow. I saw myself going a long way with the congregation, dedicating my life to the cult of the Eucharist. Though his spirituality appeared surreal and fantastic to us teenagers (there were stories of physical struggles with the devil near the end of his life), we sensed that his mission was our mission; his passion, our passion; his longing for communion with the divine body and blood, our longing. My journey actually began at the age of ten or so, when we moved to a different part of the city where we were living. Our new parish was served by the Congregation of the Blessed Sacrament. I had long cherished the idea of being a priest, and, as I entered high school, I wanted to attend junior seminary. There was something particularly engaging and meaningful about what the priests and brothers of the congregation did, especially the ritual of perpetual adoration before the exposed host. I fast became involved with parish life, first as an altar boy, and then as sacristan. I recall one brother in particular, the porter. His name was Brother Matthias. I would visit him often during the day. We would talk about his days as a missionary in Africa, and he would sometimes let me help with porter duties. I think he sensed the possibility of some religious calling in me, and I remember that he would often encourage me in subtle ways. In the porter's office, there was a black-and-white picture of Saint Eymard taken during his lifetime. He ruled over the house like a silent, talismanic ancestor.

For some reason, I recall those times with Brother Matthias as being erotically charged. Nothing ever happened, but now, some forty years later, I can better understand their true meaning. I was undergoing a rite of passage. He was my mentor, the elder of the tribe whose responsibility it was to initiate me into their secret ways. I was about to enter a very special world, a closed world of celibate men, living by rules all their own, with a clear-cut purpose. In the give-and-take of our daily conversations, he was teaching me how to be a

Blessed Sacrament religious, what our history and our legends were, and what it meant to choose such a life. If good pedagogy is, in fact, erotically based, then Brother Matthias was seducing me into my future status and training as a member of the tribe, the congregation. He often said he was praying for my vocation, so I am relatively confident that he knew exactly what he was doing in spending so many hours with me. He was angelic-looking: a generous, gentle man. He was also short, with a trim, compact body, not unattractive in his own way. It is strange that I should remember such details. Perhaps I saw him as a paternal figure. Perhaps I wanted him to do more than simply talk to me about what my future life as one of his confrères might be like.

I had several such mentors during my brief formative stay with the congregation. They were all men who took me under their wings, teaching me what I needed to know along the way, helping to nurture what they saw as a call to the priesthood: the seminary principal, the prefect of discipline, my French teacher, my history teachers, my religion teacher and future novice master, a brother who taught me how to paint. If it had not been for these adult men giving me guidance and support, my seminary experience would not have been the rich and sweet symphony that it was. Nor, I believe, would I be the gay man that I am today. Younger males need the affectionate and vigilant attention of older males in their often stormy transition to adulthood. Young gay males expect and crave similar care and regard, though these are no doubt of a different sort. During my seminary and novitiate years, I was in the daily presence of men who not only took good care of me physically and intellectually, but who also guided me spiritually, either by the force of their example or by their words. I naturally developed bonds of affection with some of them more than with others. I was learning to desire men, to feel comfortable and secure with them, to inhabit their special world with force and gentleness, to speak, walk, and think like them, to tap into their spirit and their view of the world, and to claim these as my own. All this was sustained and reaffirmed by the energy and intensity of my religious vocation. Unconsciously, and ever so quietly, I was apprenticing what it means to be a secure, confident gay man.

Mentoring is something that we must all receive and give as gay men. In coming out, I was taught sexually and culturally by older gay men. They initiated me into the arcane codes of the gay lifestyle, into its erotic possibilities, and into its spaces and its privileged moments. I have done the same in return, and in many different ways. There actually is something reassuring and quite touching about this cyclical, universal process of mentoring for those who come after us, as we were by those who went before. Often, however, we refuse to take up the responsibility, as though it were something useless and nonessential, a holdover from ancient, more closeted days. Nothing could be further from the truth. Perhaps today, more than ever, younger gay men need us to teach them our history, both the erotic and the political, our spiritual and cultural heritage, and our notions of masculinity. At a time when "being gay" seems so much more of an accepted and commonplace fact, there is wisdom in reminding ourselves and the generations to come of our painful and sad inheritance of oppression and intolerance, the better to avoid complacency. We are all repositories of cultural codes and bits of wisdom, picked up and systematized throughout the course of our lives. Part of the onus falling on us as out gay men is to transmit this collected acumen to our younger gay brothers. Not only is this a vital necessity; it also constitutes a sure and precious means of survival.

Saint Peter Julian Eymard was, for me, the ideal model of single-minded purpose and zeal. I have read several versions of his life over the years. I am always struck by a dual force in his personality: on the one hand, his total belief and confidence in his Eucharistic calling, whatever the obstacles; on the other, his willingness to trust enough in this vision to forego a comfortable and already established clerical career. He never ceased moving forward, trying to grasp, ever more clearly, the unique mission to which he felt called. In fact, all genuine saints experience this constant nudge to be someone else, while at the same time being forced to abandon whatever it is that is securely and safely holding them back. In many respects, this is a universally human experience. Saints simply assume the risk more often than the rest of us do. In the case of Saint Eymard, what is particularly striking and ultimately endearing about his life choices is the fact that they never really ceased inhabiting his spirit, playing themselves out over and over again, until the end.

There were two stories about Peter Julian as a young boy in his village of La Mure that I especially enjoyed. The first told about his habit of crouching behind the tabernacle in the empty village church talking to the Eucharistic Jesus, while his mother searched in vain for him at mealtime. Some years ago, while visiting this same church, I stood on the same spot, trying to sense the love of this young boy for his God. The second was how he had seen Napoleon, on his return from exile in Elba, marching through La Mure. This may have impressed upon the future founder a notion of the king-ship of Christ, thereby imprinting his congregation with a uniquely monarchical notion of prayerful adoration before the regally exposed host. The first story speaks to me of the pristine origins of our spiri-tuality in our childhood fixations and obsessions; the second, of the remarkable and unpredictable intersections of personal charisma and history, of contingency and fate.

The Eymardian spiritual tradition has remained with me. I still de-rive a great deal of personal meaning from the many New Testament stories and episodes focusing on the mystery of the Eucharist, and Holy Thursday is an important feast day in my liturgical life. One of my very favorite passages from the scriptures is the encounter on the road to Emmaus, from the gospel of Luke. It is not a long story, though it clearly has an air of subtle and quiet drama to it. I like it for several reasons. Two artists I am especially fond of, Caravaggio and Van Gogh, painted wonderful renditions of it. It is constructed on ambiguity and mystery, so I can look under and through it, engaging in a form of queer exegesis. It is all about physical, tactile things, about a handsome stranger, and about food: in a word, the Eucharist. It is also about three men in a room. Who knows what can happen?

This is the story from Luke's gospel.[41] Two disciples are walking along the road to Emmaus, when Jesus, unrecognized, appears among them. They are disheartened, for they had heard of the risen body of Christ which could not be found. Jesus scolds them mildly, calling them "foolish men" and "slow." He then explains the prophecies to them, presumably as a way of building links with his own ministry. Slow as they indeed were, they still did not recognize him. Evening approaches. As they near Emmaus, they press him to stay with them, the rule of hospitality requiring so. He does, and, as they sit down to eat, he breaks bread and blesses it, repeating the simple paradigmatic act of the last supper. They immediately recognize him, but he has disappeared from their sight. They then tell each other, in words that I find especially suggestive, if not downright seductive: "Did not our hearts burn within us as he talked to us on the road and explained the scriptures to us?" They return to Jerusalem to meet with the assembled apostles, who are presumably still in their state of postcrucifixion hiding. The passage ends with the following words: "They then told their story of what had happened on the road and how they had recognized him at the breaking of the bread."

This is the classic Eucharistic tale. Its beauty lies in its intimacy. Who were these two disciples? Friends? Brothers? Lovers? They appear to live together. A mysterious stranger suddenly joins them on the lonely road to Emmaus. How do they react? Though the gospel says that Jesus explained scripture to them, what else do they discuss? They ask him to share their simple room and board for the night. Do they, in fact, pick up the attractive stranger, invite him in for more than simply breaking bread? As they sit down for the evening meal, they sense something about to change as the stranger repeats the habitual Eucharistic invitation: "Take my body, eat." When they finally manage to clue in, their one recorded comment and response is of "hearts burning." This speaks to me very directly and beautifully of love and desire, of the powerful attractiveness of the unknown, of the strong and heady erotic mixture that is the enigmatic. I would venture to say that there *was* touching *on* the road to Emmaus, as well as *in* the home of these two lost and frightened disciples. I like to think that they were walking hand-in-hand on the road to Emmaus, that the arrival of the stranger only served to heighten the intensity of their attraction to each other and to him, and that the shared meal was but a prelude to something far sweeter and more desirable, something that would provide them ultimate comfort and reassurance in their dark moment of doubt and uncertainty. As the stranger suddenly disappears, after perhaps more than symbolically offering them his body to ingest, they are left in awe and gratitude, sure and confident. "Did our hearts not burn within us...?"

This is my gay version of the Road to Emmaus story. One other reason that I like it so much, apart from its inherent exegetical queerness, is because I have a gay Emmaus of my own, a tale also having to do with discreet touches and the cry for communion at the heart of unspoken desire. It is a story of three close friends, a cup of wine and some bread, and a late-night sleepover.

In my novitiate days, when I was only seventeen and preparing to launch on my chosen path as a religious with the congregation, we were always decrying the fact, as is often the prerogative of idealistic youth, that our community life was lacking in intensity. There were three of us who, no doubt because of some incorrigible enthusiasm, decided we would re-create our own sense of community. We naturally gravitated together, partly because of our personalities, but also, in hindsight, because of some unspoken sexual chemistry. I was from

Canada, and the other two came from Montana and Wisconsin. My friend from Montana and I are gay. The third friend from Wisconsin, who was really an endearing farm boy at heart, charming and with a slightly corny sense of humor, ended up as a diocesan priest, but died from some horrid brain tumor some years ago. I do not know if he was gay, but he may have been. He had one of the most perfect bodies I have ever seen on a man, no doubt due to the exertion of all that farm work. It was both an aesthetic and an erotic experience to watch him carry his frame around.

We would meet more or less regularly, often late at night, to share a Eucharist of our own. I have written elsewhere about these moments:

> We gathered in the evening in one room. Sitting on the floor and holding hands, we prayed together, and we recounted the experience of our day. We shared a reading from Scripture. A chalice and a host were placed on the floor, and one of us recited the priestly words of consecration as the other two bowed their heads. We drank and ate the body and blood, embracing one another. It is strange, when you think about it, that we should have felt the need to copy the ritual of the Catholic mass in a setting that was already heavily imbibed with such ceremonies, almost as though we were unsure of the value and validity of the real thing. We believed we were duplicating the intimacy and the conspiratorial intensity of the early Christians. When we were finished, we sometimes decided that we would "sleep over," and we would lie on the hardwood floor holding hands. There was never anything sexual about it. For us, there was a seamless fit between the eucharist we had just shared and this expression of our comradeship. It was all right; it made sense.[42]

Obviously, there are several parallels with the Emmaus story: three men, three disciples, in a room; the breaking of bread; the sharing of scripture; the search for intimacy, and community, and understanding. What I recall most vividly, however, is the tactile sense of touch that surrounded the whole event. I mean touch in the spiritual, the emotional, and the erotic sense. There were multiple and complex levels of bonding and touch between us: the friendly bonding of religious brothers in community, the bonding caused by spiritual intensity and vision, and finally, but by no means least, the bonding from desiring and desirable bodies in close proximity to each other. We chastely held hands while reciting the words of consecration, but we also did so while trying to fall asleep on the painfully hard floor. I know what my touch on the floor was about. It was, as with the Emmaus disciples, all about "burning hearts." It was about the engrossing image of my friend and brother from Wisconsin in his immaculately white briefs and chiseled chest as he got undressed. One false move, one slight shift, and my touch would have gladly turned perverse. But sad to say, it never did.

I believe there is a deep and persistent line of Eucharistic touch — jagged perhaps, but still there — extending from my modest novitiate experiment to the bright moment of revelation at Emmaus, and then back again. It is the same Eucharistic touch, the same affective connection, that links me and my dark desires to those of several of my former seminary classmates, and to members of the congregation who still carry the mark, if not the curse, of having loved other men. It is the same Eucharistic touch binding me to the Beloved Apostle leaning on the chest of Jesus at the Last Supper, or to Saint Peter Julian Eymard in ecstatic adoration alone late at night in his Parisian monastery, or to the host that I take seductively from the warm hands of the young handsome priest on a bright Sunday morning in my local parish church. "Take my body, eat. Take my blood, drink." The Eucharistic touch is always a risky one, for, as with real physical hunger and thirst, it can devour you, or cause you to devour others. Though this line of Eucharistic touch may indeed be uneven or faint in parts, it still remains boldly and deeply inscribed in my own body and blood as a sometimes wayward son of the Apostle of the Eucharist.

When working in my study, I often gaze at a photo postcard of Rodin's bust of Saint Eymard on the wall in front of me. Interestingly enough, I have recently noticed that, some years ago, I taped a small wallet size photo of my own father on the glass covering this image. I was struck the other day by this amazing juxtaposition of the two paternal figures of my life: one, the biological father; the other, the spiritual one; one, the giver of physical life; the other, the shaper of my spiritual sensibilities. This is quite an apt and fitting combination. My father, though not a particularly religious man, always spoke very proudly and affectionately of my choice to study with the Congregation of the Blessed Sacrament. He liked the priests from our parish, and I do recall that they were particularly good to us, and to him no doubt, when my mother died. Beyond this surface link, however, there stirs the far deeper meaning of how my own father and Peter Julian Eymard have fashioned and molded me, very much in their image and likeness. Though I may be the gay son of one, and the renegade son of the other, I still owe both men the lineage of my body and soul. My father, unawares, taught me desire, the love of men; Eymard, devotion, the obsession with the divine body. In a way, they inhabit the same country; each is parent to the other. Upon my mother's death, I left my father to run to Saint Peter Julian, and I returned to my father when I abandoned the safety of the founder's mantle. If it had not been for both, the cycle of my journey would have been incomplete. As a mature gay man, I still look to Eymard with a mixture of gratitude and filial respect. It was his congregation and his disciples who molded and inspired me. In the same way, my biological father influenced and encouraged me to walk my own path. I eventually moved on from both, only to rediscover and appreciate each anew. Unmistakably, this cyclic journey is a son's — all sons' — necessary odyssey, gay sons especially so.

Several years ago, while touring the south of France, I visited Saint Peter Julian Eymard's hometown of La Mure. Naturally, this spiritual experience was very moving and meaningful. I had always wanted to go there. Some years before that, I had returned to the site of the novitiate I attended in central Massachusetts, now a Buddhist meditation center. A sense of place connecting me to my past is important to me. These were sacred locales, sites of meaning and power. Whenever I enter a church or sanctuary staffed by the Blessed Sacrament Fathers, such as the ones in Montreal, or particularly New York where I spent a portion of my training, I immediately feel reconnected, reaffirmed, rerooted. I would especially like to return to my minor seminary, now belonging, so I've been told, to a sect. What would I look for? Not the chapel, or the classrooms, or the study hall. Rather, I would haunt the dormitories, showers, locker rooms, and outside playing fields where I recall gawking at my classmates, younger and older, in all their physical splendor. It was in these sacred places that I encountered the Real Presence.

Take my body, eat. Take my blood, drink. Peter Julian Eymard ingested wholly, spending the Eucharistic force in and upon me, teaching me to want the divine presence.

Blessed Peter Julian Eymard, lover of the body and blood of the Savior, spiritual father and guide, continue teaching me to commune with the Eucharistic mystery. As I touch and swallow the bodies of other men, help me to see the source of my love in the divine person of Jesus, the most perfect and desirable of all men. Grant us solace, give us zeal, bestow your Eucharistic passion upon our weary, wandering souls. Teach us to pray, as you prayed and stood guard over your King in the early morning hours. I will always return to your gentle and confident example. Instill in me a never-ending thirst for the body of my Lord. Amen.

ELEVEN

The Erotic Christ

I BEGIN WRITING THIS CHAPTER on Christmas Day. At first look, it may appear strange, if not slightly perverse, to reflect on the erotic Christ on the day of his birth as an infant. In fact, if the mystery of the Incarnation means anything at all, it certainly means that God became fully man, and this includes the erotic life. Though the debate continues to rage as to whether Jesus was a fully sexual being, my intent is not to contribute further to the polemic. I take it for granted that he was, otherwise he would not and could not have been such an exceptional human creature. Rather, I wish to contemplate the figure of the Christ as a source of erotic desire and, occasionally, fulfillment. As I glance at the countless images and statues, especially that of the almost naked, muscular man hanging on a wooden cross, silently inviting my contemplation, I also recognize his attractiveness as a powerful source of homoerotic longing. I have no doubt that my very first religious palpitations were intensely caught up subconsciously with this desirable figure of a man, just as I am certain they still are. In the panoply of male holy figures, that of Jesus holds a place of honor and passion.

This experience can be a rather common one for gay men growing up in Catholic environments, where the crucified figure of the Christ often dominates one's visual field, including the home and the school. Catholic popular piety also imitates the trappings and inner dynamics of erotic attraction. Theologian Robert E. Goss writes affectionately of his days as a Jesuit novice in *Queering Christ: Beyond*

Jesus Acted Up, when prayer, for him, became an act of seduction, but where it was also a source of mixed messages.

> In prayer, I imagined a naked Jesus as a muscular, handsome bearded man embracing me and became sexually aroused. I envisioned burying my face in his hair-matted chest, and I found myself fighting off sexual fantasies. Catholic asceticism aimed at repressing sexual impulses, maintaining flaccid penises, and creating lifeless bodies, but Catholic piety stimulated an erotic love for Jesus. Catholic asceticism introduced a monastic discipline of the flaccid penis while Catholic piety transformed ascetic practices into an erotic stimulation of the penis. Only several years later was I able to sort out this contradiction between the asceticism of the flaccid penis and a piety stimulating the penis.[43]

Goss's remarks point to the disjunction that can often exist between how we are *taught* to understand Jesus, and how we, in fact, *experience* him as gay men. It is made abundantly clear, though certainly never directly, that our penis should never enter into the equation. After all, Jesus is God, and the genital organs are not a proper instrument of prayer to a god (they conveniently forget a certain history of priapic worship). The problem comes up, so to speak, when the penis comes up, both literally and metaphorically.

I retain one strong memory from my very early childhood, about the age of four or so. I remember being alone in a room, no doubt lying or sitting in my crib. The walls were made of wood. I glanced at the window, and I saw a huge lion growling back at me. At that point, suddenly, my mother walked into the room. I am not really sure what happened. Was it simply some terrible childish nightmare? Was I experiencing some intense infantile sexual projection? Was there really a lion on the loose in the town where we lived? Years later, when I was thinking of becoming a psychotherapist and undergoing my first mandatory therapy session, I recounted this story to my therapist. I subsequently abandoned this project, but the therapist, a classic older Freudian, took the time to write me a letter encouraging me to explore, in much greater depth, this episode of the lion. Obviously, for him it was foundational in my life, the source of some deep-seated sexual perversion or neurosis.

I was not particularly afraid of the lion; more fascinated than fearful. In looking back upon this incident, I like to think of the lion figure as symbolic of an important and essential feature of my inner psyche, namely the lure and erotic power of maleness. In this sense, the portrait of the lion, whatever may have been the precise circumstances of the childhood event in question, stands as a paradigmatic image and energy in my life, in ways often unbidden and mysterious. I think the icon of the crucified Christ operates in much the same way. For as long as I can recall, I have had a special enthrallment with the Christian *corpus*. The body of the crucified Jesus, intensely desirable in its plundered and suffering masculinity, beckons me by the sheer power of its homoerotic enticement. In my psychological as in my spiritual inner landscape, the lion and the Christ are really one and the same. Superbly charged images of masculine strength and beauty, they each shatter and possess me. I can only bow in submission and veneration before their sweet, ineffable grace. Weak-kneed and compliant, I willingly submit to their soothing ravages.

In reality, the lion and the Christ carry different, though complementary, aspects of a single personality. The lion represents brute aggressive force, the male as dominant energy and the definite top. The crucified Jesus, on the other hand, elicits strong feelings of comfort and passive submission, the male as docile and compliant bottom. In the gay male erotic experience, both embody the possibility of transcendent and generous giving, because both can be transformed, at any point, into a moment of intimate grace. Catholic scripts of pious devotion, whether it be to saints or to the man-god

Jesus himself, play on the ambivalence and mutuality of the dominant and the submissive. I want and need to be taken and possessed by the saint or by the Christ, but I also want and need to take and possess him: to make him my own; or me, to be made into his own, to paraphrase a well-loved hymn. Certainly nothing about flaccid penises here, only a generous and liberating tumescence.

Worshiping the handsomely glorious body of Jesus hung from the cross, gay men can enter into an act of erotic and spiritual intimacy with their lord. As they kneel and bring their gaze upward, they see suspended in front of them, inviting in his seminaked vulnerability, his arms open wide to embrace them, the broken and desirable body of the one who was all things to all people, the source of their need, and truly its ultimate fulfillment. This need to commune with the physical body of Jesus, or with any of its sacred parts, shares in a long-standing tradition of Christian mysticism. One need only think of the opposite- or same-sex erotic imagery of Saints Teresa of Avila and John of the Cross, or the stories of ecstatic medieval nuns communing with the radiantly glorified foreskin of Jesus in fits of religious rapture. Such moments of erotic grace and revelation symbolize intimate divine-human congress, but they also elevate the human person to the status of sacred consort, to the role and position of the divine object of desire. There can be great power in such imagery, and there can be especially great power if the person is socially and culturally marginal: a woman or a homosexual, for example. Intimate union with the divine, a privileged access to the holy, bestows communal and spiritual stature, just as it engenders a form of personal wholeness: acceptance in the eyes of God; desired and touched by God; summoned forth by God's love. As gay men fix their tearful eyes on the crucified Jesus, infinitely desirable in his gashed and vulnerable beauty, they find themselves transfigured into his spiritual partners, and they can imagine themselves one in and with him, lovers in a dangerous time.

Robert Goss summarizes such feelings in these words: "I and many other Catholic men, priests and laymen, have found the naked Jesus utterly sexually desirable, calling us to pursue a relationship, and many of us have discovered that we were utterly desirable to Jesus."[44] Christian homodevotion to Jesus, to use his expression, has a long and honored pedigree, and has included a variety of different theological conceptions and devotional approaches.[45] It has also functioned as a positive venue for gay men in appropriating for themselves the central tenets and imagery of the Christian spiritual tradition, though very often in the guise of more orthodox religious language. This process, as Goss points out, is a dynamic one: we find Jesus desirable, but, in turn, we find ourselves desirable in his sight. As gay men, we are thereby reaffirmed and confirmed in our basic humanity, but also in our sexuality. Though this may seem fairly obvious, it can assume a revolutionary dimension in the context of an openly homophobic religious tradition such as Catholicism, for example. Homodevotion, whether subtle or blatant, to the paradigmatic figure of the Christ subverts and destabilizes many religious claims over our bodies and our lives. In embracing the broken body of Jesus, in all its precious parts, we also embrace and begin to heal our own broken and spurned bodies. Bodies are really what devotion is all about: hungry, desperate bodies; bodies in the throes of passionate physical union and prayerful ecstasy; bodies caressed, anointed, and embraced; bodies adored, cuddled, and worshiped. The language of spiritual devotion is not much different from that of human love, if perhaps only in degrees.

I try to remember, as a youth and as a young adult in the seminary, the nature of my relationship with the figure of Jesus. My world was replete with it, from the home to the school, and most certainly in church. His body and face were everywhere, sometimes smiling and effeminate, the Good Shepherd or the captain of my ship, or more

generally in the form of the suffering and crucified God. My boyhood notions of the body of Jesus, as hazy and uncertain as they
were, remained tied up with pietistic visions of an ethereal being, but
also, in an ironic way, with the warm and strong paternal body of the
father, a body I intensely desired but that remained taboo. I curiously
suspect that, in my childlike simplicity, my father and Jesus were one
and the same person. There was also the body of the child or adolescent Jesus, the one lost in the temple or standing between his parents
in any number of versions of the Holy Family. Could this Jesus be my
friend? Did this Jesus have a penis? Could he show me? Why not? I
saw my brother's. Why not his? Actually, this young Jesus was rather
sexless, more a source of curious fantasy than the willing companion
of my emerging erotic needs.

When I prayed in church as a youngster, I liked to dwell on
thoughts of the blood of Jesus. It was the only one of his bodily fluids (were/could there be any others?) that I could visualize, no doubt
because it was the only one figured in the iconography of the cross.
I subconsciously knew there had to be others, notably sperm, but
I could not imagine them because of an overpowering taboo about
such things. The imagery of the saving blood of Christ was, and still
is, found everywhere in Catholic liturgical texts and hymns. One of
my favorites is the Lenten hymn, "O Sacred Head Surrounded." Not
only is it melodiously beautiful, but it describes in vivid detail the
sorrowful condition of Christ's body in the course of his passion.
For a pious gay youth, thoughts of thick blood gushing from that
most holy and precious of all male bodies obviously refers to other
even more desirable fluids springing forth in copious amounts. I no
doubt wanted the sperm of Jesus, the mark of his unfailing affection,
to cover me and save me just as his holy blood did. Catholic devotion
to the Precious Blood has always fascinated me. In the city where I
lived before entering the seminary, there was an order of contemplative nuns dedicated to the cult of the Precious Blood. I wanted to be

one of them, in their striking white and red robes, endlessly adoring the sacred liquid.

In pre-AIDS days, the exchange of blood was a sure sign of intimate and lasting commitment. Just as boys might become blood brothers by the mixing of their red fluid, or soldiers even closer companions simply by having it surround and immerse their world so copiously, my contemplating the blessed blood of Jesus created a bond of affinity and reciprocity between me and him. I could imagine it anointing me and entering me, filling me and cleansing me. This blood of Jesus circumscribed my world, accessible through his crucified figure, the Good Friday liturgy, or any number of prayers, supplications, and litanies. But this blood was a surrogate liquid, not the thing really desired, for it was not the nectar of erotic exchange. Blood was not what I truly craved in the intimacy of my unspoken obsession. It was the divine seed, the most perfect sign of the most perfect communion from that most perfect of all male bodies, for which I ached. I wanted to ingest and retain this host, so that it could make me his now and forever. It was as though this were all I needed to become the person I suspected I was, the boy not quite like all the others, but the one Jesus understood and accepted. How better to seal this very special friendship than by the exchange of what only males can produce?

Speaking of semen and the body of Jesus carries a blasphemous risk in the eyes of some. Yet, is there anything more precious, more life-affirming and generous, even in these days of infection, than the human male sperm? If Jesus was fully human, as church teaching says he was, then he certainly possessed semen, and, if his body was as much a biological entity as yours or mine, which it no doubt was, then he must have evacuated it every now and then. Perhaps he even shared it with some others in moments of pleasurable familiarity. For gay men, such an image is anything but sacrilegious. It remakes Jesus into the desirable male that he was, fully possessed of his generative capacity, and able to use it as the sign and actuality of his intimate communion with others. To enter a level of deep companionship with this Jesus implies an exchange of bodily fluids: ours, the saliva, tears, and occasional blood of our suppliant prayers; his, the redemptive blood, water, and semen of his sacred person. For gay men especially, exchanging sperm is an intense and profoundly erotic act, one expressive of a powerfully masculine urge, and of the need to claim same-sex pleasure as one's own. "The exchange of semen is often experienced as a vital expression of intimacy; for gay male relationships it becomes a signifier of powerful intimacy and human connection, a defiance of the procreative privilege of normative heterosexuality; and an expression of our freedom."[46] There is a certain glorious anarchy to this defiantly nonprocreative spilling of seed. Between gay men, as between the lone believer and his God, it contains the hope and promise of desire fulfilled.

The Christ-body of my minor seminary and novitiate years was of a different sort, though he retained his fine masculine energy and presence. Because ours was foremost a cult of the Eucharistic mysteries, he inhabited the elements of bread and wine, somewhat hidden beneath their ordinary-looking surfaces. His was a body to be shared with others and ingested: the promise and the sign of our community life. His was a liturgical body, exposed in the monstrance, a body to be saluted and adored. But I do recall his presence in other ways: in the dominant ubiquity of the priests and brothers — bodies always on the verge of claiming and subsuming ours — and in the naked and sweaty grace of my fellow seminarians: bodies close and dangerous, but so excessively and needlessly desirable. I knew nothing of sex, but I saw penises around me every day. I imagined penises under black cassocks, and I masturbated to their imaginary forms. I glimpsed and occasionally gawked at erect penises under dormitory pajamas, and they fed my solitary ministrations. The Eucharistic Jesus did not visibly have a penis, imprisoned as he was in the material species, but his ministers and devotees certainly did. They were his surrogates, and they defined the erotic space and temperament of my spiritually formative years. Their sexual organs circumscribed my world.

But Jesus did have a penis, just as he had blood and semen. How many Christian gay men have not glanced at an image of the crucified or dead Christ, and silently asked themselves what this penis looked like? Its length and width? Its texture and hue? No doubt it was circumcised, as was culturally and religiously appropriate for a Jew. In fact, the historical Jesus would have been crucified naked, a further sign of his humiliation as a common criminal. The passion portal of the Sagrada Familia temple in Barcelona, in a massive sculpture by Subirachs, shows a naked crucified Christ, his imposing rock penis hanging in view of all, forcing us to admire and fear its latent virility. This human penis of Jesus, whether or not it was ever used sexually, reaffirms, in the most visible and human way possible, the complete gift of the Creator through the Incarnation. In his masterful study of the genitalia of Christ in Renaissance art, Leo Steinberg writes:

> The eternal, by definition, experiences neither death nor generation. If the godhead incarnates itself to suffer a human fate, it takes on the condition of being both deathbound and sexed. The mortality it assumes is correlative with sexuality, since it is by procreation that the race, though consigned to death individually, endures collectively to fulfill the redemptive plan. Therefore, to profess that God once embodied himself in a human nature is to confess that the eternal, there and then, became mortal and sexual. Thus understood, the evidence of Christ's sexual member serves as the pledge of God's humanation.[47]

Though its worship is neglected in Catholic devotional strategies for reasons of sexual fear and discomfort, the penis of Jesus, as with all his other bodily parts, should rightly possess a proper cult of its own.

The phallus as a life-giving symbol of fertility extends back into the mists of human history. I can see a courageous band of gay believers, keen and committed phallic missionaries, advocating and spreading a special devotion to the holy genitals of Jesus. A questionable medieval fantasy perhaps, but one certainly no more suspicious than any of the others centered on sacred blood, wounds, foreskins, and other physical scars and organs, to say nothing of the suffering divine body as a whole.

A glorious example of a fully male, genitally endowed figure of Jesus the Christ is Michelangelo's powerfully denuded sculpture of the *Risen Christ*. When I first saw the original in a Roman church, I was shocked and saddened by the fact that its genital area, out of misplaced false modesty, had been covered with some metallic loincloth. When I admired the uncovered body in a photograph, I was stunned. It is a classically rich and aesthetically uplifting piece, an homage by the homosexual Michelangelo to masculine beauty and perfection. I recall walking around the statue, admiring the muscular arms, thighs, and buttocks, but regrettably unable to peer underneath its out-of-place underwear at the proper manly endowment of the risen Jesus. I simply failed to comprehend the sad, perverse logic that had thought it right to spoil the artist's brilliance. No doubt the most engaging element about this wonderful piece of work is how it brings together the notions of pristine innocence and bodily integrity, of how full humanity is not bad or ugly, but the fine manifestation of some intense and deep divine splendor. Again, in the words of Leo Steinberg:

> But the intended nudity of Michelangelo's figure was neither a licentious conceit nor thoughtless truckling to antique example. If Michelangelo denuded his *Risen Christ,* he must have sensed a rightness in his decision more compelling than inhibitions of modesty; must have seen that a loincloth would convict these genitalia of being "pudenda," thereby denying the very work

of redemption which promised to free human nature from its Adamic contagion of shame.

… We must, I think, credit Michelangelo with the knowledge that Christian teaching makes bodily shame no part of man's pristine nature, but attributes it to the corruption brought on by sin. And would not such Christian knowledge direct him to the ideality of antique sculpture? Where but in ancient art would he have found the pattern of naked perfection untouched by shame, nude bodies untroubled by modesty? Their unabashed freedom conveyed a possibility which Christian teaching reserved only for Christ and for those who would resurrect in Christ's likeness: the possibility of a human nature without human guilt.[48]

And, yes, how indeed, but from the gifted and gentle hand of a same-sex loving sculptor?

I discovered a different erotic Christ during my formative novitiate years, that of the slightly pantheistic Jesuit mystic Pierre Teilhard de Chardin. In the heyday of 1960s' cultural renewal, his works, once banned by the church as theologically suspect because they were too close to evolutionary science, were experiencing a renaissance, particularly amongst young and idealistic seminarians like me.[49] Teilhard de Chardin's scientific work can be cumbersome and fairly inaccessible, relatively uninteresting in fact, but his theological reflections were sheer poetry. Apart from the beauty of his language, what most struck me about his writings was his concern with the body of the cosmic Christ. Teilhard de Chardin was a staunch evolutionist, but he believed that humans are evolving spiritually as well as biologically, and that increased evolutionary sophistication necessarily implies an increased spiritual awareness, until we finally merge with Christ himself at the omega point. For Teilhard, the entire natural cosmos is the body of Christ, and we are "evolving ourselves," biologically and spiritually, into that body. The pantheistic dimensions of his thinking, often overemphasized by Catholic orthodoxy for reasons of inquisitorial bluff, are relatively obvious. He has also been accused, unfairly so, of a form of scientific and theological simplicity, of a misplaced romanticism about the natural world.

In my perhaps naive frame of mind as a young seminarian, I found Teilhard's idea that we are all part of Christ's cosmic body, ever increasing in size and complexity, to be an intensely attractive and erotically charged one: we are all making love together, all the time, down through history and far into the distant future, and doing so as different parts of Christ's body, who is loving himself eternally. We are participating in an evolutionary cosmic orgy. I recall one of Teilhard's writings where he describes celebrating a mass "over the world," because he did not have the elements of bread and wine at his disposal to do so properly. If this world is, in fact, the body of Christ, then consecrating and offering up its various parts as a sign of the sacrificial testament becomes an act of mystical insight. This richly suggestive notion of a physical, embodied Christ permeating all of natural creation, and consequently every single created being — a concept not all that theologically unusual — opened up wonderful vistas for me. Now, every human encounter was transformed potentially into a moment of physical convergence. Every touch carried the promise of transcendence. Every body rightly became a holy body, an integral part of the overarching mystical body. And every intoxicatingly desirable male body could be none other than the cosmic Christ's body.

In meditating on the life of Jesus, on those times when his body awakens desire in me, I am carried back to four "hidden" or silent episodes: to the young adult in Nazareth, the time in the wilderness prior to his public ministry, the descent from the cross, and the lying entombed before his glorious resurrection. In a way, each situation was formative, conditional, uncertain. Each could have gone either way. Above all, each remains linked with a unique bodily predicament, with how Jesus was in the world, and with how he still continues to question and summon us.

I see a nineteen-year-old Jesus coming into his adult prime, working as an eager apprentice in his father Joseph's carpentry shop. A handsome man, he is the pride of his parents. Caring and attentive, sensitive yet principled, he has been known to turn the head of many a Nazareth girl, but also of a few young men. I am one of those. I find him sexy beyond all measure. When I glimpse him working bare-chested in the burning sun, I cannot help but stare, hoping that he might look up and smile. One day, it happens. We begin to talk. He likes me. We fast become friends, and I feel increasingly that my life would be nothing without him. I look for opportunities to touch him, be with him, place my hand upon his shoulder, affectionately play with his hair. He lets me. Some months later, in the silence of a starry night, I become his. I will choose to follow him.

I see a swarthy thirty-year-old Jesus, alone for forty days with Satan in the dry and savage heat of a Palestinian desert. I am the devil. This truly exceptional man disturbs me, not because he claims he may be the son of that bloodthirsty tribal god, but because his rugged, emaciated body makes me quiver quite madly with desire. Alone, I think I may be able to seduce him. I offer him all the riches and power I can possibly summon, but he continues to resist, calm and composed in his brazen certainties. I grow angry and restless. I must have him. Shall I simply take him, possess him, discard him? Yet I, who am usually so adept at getting my way with humans, find myself inexplicably powerless. I am obsessed. I decide to bide my time. This Jesus, this very human man, will have to die sooner or later, like all the others. At that moment, I will rush to claim him as mine.

I crouch at the foot of the cross as the broken and bloody body of Jesus is laid in my arms. I am the beloved disciple, the special friend, the one with whom he wanted to share his life. How beautiful you still look in your suffering and pain, my love, my sweet man, my eternal life. How much I have stroked and enjoyed your precious body. How I will miss not lying in the warmth and secure comfort of your gentle embrace. I kiss you tenderly. My tears wash away the caked blood and dried spit on your arms and face. I will miss you so, so much, devoid as I will be of any purpose for existing. You were my universe, my morning and night, my all. I carefully wash the still warm dead body of my beloved, kissing him again and again, cleansing the open wounds with my hopeless cries. Why, O God, why have you done this to him, your son, my lover?

I see the dead body of Jesus laid out in the eerie silence of the nearly empty tomb. I am the guard stationed in front of the cavern opening, and told to beware of half-crazed disciples and other lunatics who may want to steal the corpse and claim that this man rose from the dead; as though this were in any way possible, humanly or otherwise. I clearly remember this man when he preached, and how his soothing words and presence fed my night-time thoughts and desires, alone in my barracks. I glance inside. There, silently, the moon casting its gentle glow over him lies the man they call Jesus, the Christ. I want to go and stand near him, perhaps kneel at his side and delicately whisper soft words of ardor and supplication in his ears. I know he will be listening, for I believe. I believe that his glory will soon dawn, that he will live again, and that I will someday die for him.

The erotic Christ is the Christ of all burning dreams and fantasies, the desire of all desires, the beauty of all beauties, the one who empties himself in me, the lord of love.

Gentle Jesus, beloved lover, keeper of my heart and soul, I come before you in the stillness of night, alone and afraid, and ask that you bathe me in your light. Keep me in your warm and soft embrace. Seize me with your might. Make me yours. I open myself up to your wondrous and soothing fire. As you send forth your spirit upon me, grant that its cool and penetrating balm heals and nourishes my broken and voracious desires for you. I beg you, dear Lord, make me whole in your wholeness, loving in your love, strong in your strength, holy in your holiness. I offer you the unending pangs and sorrows of all my cherished gay brothers. We who have loved and desired you, we the outcasts, gather us together in your wondrous and secure arms. Show us the true glory and beauty of your face. Touch us that we may touch you. O heavenly and bounteous lover, make us your own, that we may never hunger after another. Amen.

TWELVE

Gay Saints

I N AUGUST 2002, my partner and I went on a Baltic cruise. We visited Russia, the former Baltic republics, and parts of Scandinavia. One of our stops was Riga, the capital of present-day Latvia. There, we visited Saint John's Church, a modest former Dominican monastery dedicated to Saint John the Baptist, but now of the Lutheran faith. It is an attractive, though by no means spectacular, church. What fascinated me most about visiting it was an unusual story I had read about what had happened there while it was still functioning as a Dominican monastic house in the Middle Ages. It seems that two young monks, in their penitential zeal to become saints, had themselves entombed while still alive behind a wall near the main altar, where they lived out their days together in prayerful contemplation, all the while being fed by their brother monks through a small opening in the wall. Their skeletal remains are still there, and a plaque marks the holy spot. Call it an unhealthy obsession with saints, or perhaps an uncanny ability to see same-sex desire wherever it points itself, but this tale engrossed me. Unfortunately, no details are available. My imagination filled in the gaps.

I imagine that these two young Latvian friars were homosexual, that they were, in fact, deeply attracted to each other, but that, because of their vows, they felt unable to express their need and their love. I imagine that, in their quest for companionship and a more perfect spiritual life, and with the full understanding and active support of their monastic brothers, they agreed to commit themselves *as a couple,* to this unusual form of bodily mortification. I imagine that they were able to create a somewhat cozy though Spartan home in their walled-up space, engaging themselves with the daily cycle of monastic contemplation. I imagine that they attained the heights of mystical experience, nurtured by prayer and penance. But above all, I imagine that, at some point, somehow, they desired and partook of each other's body, giving free rein to their erotic hunger one for the other, and that this experience became an intense and fruitful source of religious and contemplative illumination. I imagine that they were given the spiritual powers of healing and prophecy, were respected far and wide as sage healers and seers, and that they died only days from each other. In their time, they were publicly regarded as saints, but the institutional church, having caught wind of their particular sexual proclivities, squelched any attempts at formal canonization. There they still lie behind that severe church wall, their bones entwined forever, two sodomite-saints.

This may be read as a wonderfully fantastic story, and, in many ways, it is. But it could also be true. Such lives, real or imagined, as romantic as we may picture them to be, can serve as inspiring templates for the amazingly rich diversity and sheer tenacity of gay people. Nothing is known about these two Latvian Dominican monks, so my story could well be within the realm of the possible. The important thing is not what I may have invented about them, or about their relationship or spirituality, but the fact that two unknown medieval monks, who I think were homosexual, have touched me across time, me a twenty-first-century gay man. It is irrelevant whether they ever saw themselves as being homosexual in their identity. I resonated so strongly to their story, as sketchy as it is, because we share a common frame of reference, at once sexual and spiritual. And in telling this story and sharing this fantasy, I have made it possible for you, the reader, to touch them in their quiet wall space, and they, you. Gay sanctity. I do believe it can be found everywhere, and in all guises.

Gay saints not only haunt our dreams and visions; they also walk the corridors of established power, though always slightly subversively.

In the early centuries of Christendom, sanctity was something acquired, a mark of respect freely given by Christian believers, very often quite localized, in recognition of an individual's outstanding holiness or special spiritual significance to the community. To be known as a saint, either whilst still alive or at the moment of one's death, was a mark of confidence and respect on the part of your fellow humans. Only considerably later, in an attempt to control what it saw as a parallel form of popular religiosity, and therefore something quite beyond its immediate control, did the institutional church formalize the process of saint-making, better known as canonization. Saints, while still powerfully engaging and holy individuals, henceforth became "official" models of the virtuous life and of submission, and therefore quite "safe" in any challenge they might pose to the rigid hegemony of a staunchly clerical structure. The saints in this book are all properly certified holy men (or boys) in the Catholic Church's hagiographic tradition and liturgical calendar. The twists that I may have put upon their lives and legends are those of a postmodern gay man, who is conversant with both Catholic culture and homoerotic desire as sites of potential transgression. Hence my queering of male sanctity.

Queering canonical saints is one thing; claiming sanctity for the great number of uncanonized is quite another, especially if they happen to be faggots. Yet I would like to propose just that, reclaiming, as it were, the popular tradition of communal saint-making. I am not suggesting, directly or indirectly, that my choices for gay sainthood should ever be canonized in any solemn or conventional sense, even though they may indeed be quite meritorious, virtuous, or heroic in their everyday lives. I would rather like to propose a schematic way of looking at our own history, a model for understanding human greatness as it has emerged, and still does, amongst ourselves. For that is exactly what saints are: ordinary human beings who have done extraordinary things, and who, in so doing, have blazed new paths of human merit and accomplishment. I will borrow, for my purposes, elements of the church's own schema of types of saints: martyrs, confessors, and doctors.

Martyrs are witnesses. They stand for certain ideals, certain important values and principles. In religious terms, they die for the faith. In the contemporary world, at least, the idea of martyrdom — of being killed for a cause — has attained a measure of secular credibility, very often having to do with political or social struggles of one particular sort or another. Depending on one's ideological or political allegiances, significant historical figures such as Che Guevera, Robert or John F. Kennedy, Martin Luther King Jr., or Stephen Biko could all be considered martyrs. In some examples closer to us, such as Palestinian suicide bombers, the ideal of martyrdom is a far more complex and controversial reality. Martyrs, in fact, can be either of the left or of the right. They can be claimed by all sides, or by none. There is another category of modern martyrs: the innocent victims of state power or culturally conditioned hatred and ostracism. Those who died in the Holocaust are one of the more compelling of such illustrations. From this perspective, martyrdom is invariably equated with blamelessness. People were eliminated because another group of people, or at times a single individual, did not like them simply for being what they were: women, children, or members of some social or cultural minority. Martyrdom is death loaded with an extreme public significance.

Gay men, by virtue of their marginal social positioning throughout history, and in many different cultural contexts, have long been the helpless victims of unbridled state or religious power structures. We have long been martyrs, very convenient and expendable scapegoats. Whether it be those who were burned on the pyres in the

Middle Ages, those used for medical experimentation in Nazi concentration camps, those left behind to die in the early years of the AIDS scare because of political and medical neglect, those still executed in Islamic countries for the so-called crime of sodomy, or those beaten savagely by thugs on a drunken Saturday night in any North American city: all, in fact, are martyrs. They all carry, on their bodies and in our souls, the mark of the martyr, of the person hated and destroyed simply for existing. In their martyrdom, they become the living symbols of our survival. One such symbol has emerged in our time, a young martyred gay man whose death galvanized the world. Interestingly enough, the process by which he attained such posthumous stature was akin to canonization by popular consent. His name was Matthew Shepard.

You may recall my story in the introduction about how I stumbled upon the idea of writing a book about saints. I was listening to an academic paper about Matthew Shepard as a saintly icon. Some objected to such a characterization as disempowering; others, on the contrary, claimed it was very powerful, fully consistent with the Catholic tradition of attainable human sanctity. It is precisely this attainability that characterizes Matthew Shepard's sudden accession to gay sainthood. His story is paradigmatic in its simplicity. Five years ago, in October 1998, a twenty-one-year-old gay University of Wyoming student was found almost dead, tied to a fence on the outskirts of a small town named Laramie. He had been beaten and pistol whipped, and left almost naked in the autumn chill. He died in hospital a few short days later. His death, funeral, and the subsequent trial of the two men accused of killing him focused world attention on homophobia and hate crimes. Numerous books and articles were written about him; films and plays were made about his life and the aftermath to his death.[50] From being a nobody, an obscure, unknown young gay man, Matthew Shepard became, in his death, an intensely powerful and engaging symbol of gay affirmation. His life appears to have been ordinary and publicly uneventful. His death assumed all the qualities and inherent contradictions of martyrdom. He became a reference point in gay cultural history, and a religious symbol of quasi-universal import.

Many factors contributed to such a transformation. Matthew Shepard was relatively young, quite boyish looking. There still hung an aura of innocence and chaste simplicity about him. Though he was no doubt a sexually active gay man (this obvious fact is seldom, if ever, mentioned, as though it might taint his larger-than-life image), and that homoerotic desire may have played some tangled part in his last few hours on earth, his sexuality became rarified, angelic, immaculate in its potency. It is interesting to note, for example, that the alleged gang rape by three men that he endured while traveling in Northern Africa is never discussed in terms of mutuality or reciprocity. This would be taboo. An especially meaningful element in this sudden metamorphosis to sainthood was the response of Matthew Shepard's parents to their son's killers. They spoke out against the death penalty for the perpetrators, and his mother launched a very public campaign against homophobia. In this way, the martyred boy himself became all-forgiving and just, a source of grace and redemption rather than a sign of hatred and revenge. His death was further ennobled by the act of forgiveness of his parents. Finally, and visually quite significant, there is the physical site and manner of his death. He was tied to a wooden fence, taunted, tortured, left to die in his own blood. The parallels are obvious, as are the images evoked. All of us can visualize the broken, bloody body of Matthew Shepard in his underwear hanging on a fence made of wood, and see, at the same moment, the dying body of Christ, in a loincloth, nailed to a wooden cross. Saints copy their God.

In his death, Matthew Shepard crossed the barrier keeping mere mortals from the heavenly host. In a secular society where religious symbols and images no longer carry the weight and import they once did, the transformation of this anonymous, martyred gay boy into an iconic figure of almost mythical proportions speaks eloquently to the need for spiritual vision. For gay men, he holds a place of honor, the sexual victim on whose sad and abused body are inscribed all of our deepest fears and unspoken longings. We have made him Saint Matthew Shepard, Martyr, for that is what we need him to be. That is how we can truly make sense of his irrational, terrifying death.

A second traditional category of saints is that of the "confessor," defined in the Oxford dictionary as "one who confesses; one who avows his religion in face of danger, but does not suffer martyrdom." The witness of the confessor is of a different sort than that of the martyr: more sustained, less dramatic, certainly equally risky. All martyrs are confessors, though not all confessors become martyrs. Though the title is not really used anymore in the Catholic tradition, some of its greatest saints were confessors: Saint Francis Xavier, King Edward the Confessor, Blessed Pius IX, to name only three. In many ways, the confessors are the stalwart workers, the ones who sustain and nurture the faith in the face of internal and external adversity. In this process, they certainly put their lives on the proverbial line, though they are not rewarded with the palm of martyrdom. Their witnessing, stubborn and resilient as it is, can often inspire others in attaining their own heroic heights. All the founders and foundresses of religious congregations, the altruistic and adventurous missionaries, the originators of holy works and social welfare programs, the modest priests, sisters, and brothers: all these saints, in fact, are exemplary in their humble and sometimes dramatic life testimonials. They can all teach us human dignity.

I claim the saintly status of the confessor for all those brave men and women, the fearless drag queens above all, who stood at Stonewall in 1969. I also claim it for the courageous gay men who continue to love their own sex under conditions of criminality and terror, whether it be in Iran, Zimbabwe, Saudi Arabia, or China. I call

Oscar Wilde a holy confessor as he stood destroyed and alone on the witness stand, boldly affirming our unnamed, unspoken love. And I address and claim all the others: the clerically ostracized in their monastic cells and rectories, the imprisoned at Dachau, the tortured and exiled at every sad twist and turn of history, the blackmailed and professionally broken in 1950s' Cold War America, the HIV-positive men imprisoned and gagged in present-day Cuba. I cry out in anger, and shock, and deep and lasting affection. I reach out to touch, ever so respectfully, their broken bodies, minds, and spirits. Strong men of promise and worth, men whose only crime was to love others like them, men compelling us to stand upright with them in bearing witness to the beauty and worth of such love. Men confessing to their desires, claiming them proudly and defiantly. Men who deserve to be called saints.

In my own life, I have known such men. They were the classmates others chose to tease and reject because they were just a bit too effeminate, not manly enough to run and jump like the rest of the boys. They were the bachelor uncles and cousins whose secret lives were sources of titillation and wildly vicarious pleasures. They were the mysterious neighbor who spent such suspiciously long periods of time alone, and who was always so nice to us boys. They were the well-mannered, impeccably dressed coworker who never went out with girls, but who was always so friendly with them. They were the graduate student, teacher, and colleague who just had to be gay because, well, he obviously was so polite, classy, and smart, and he had such perfectly exquisite taste. They were the brother you could call sissy because you did not really like him, and he simply spent too much time playing house. They were all the boys and men who simply could not, or did not want to, play by the rules of an oppressively heterosexual culture. And I and others have been every single one of those men at certain times in our lives, proud confessors in our own right.

The confessing act, as with the act of martyrdom, is one of simple yet visionary courage. Some become martyrs by default, while others remain confessors by default. In both cases, however, choice is inevitably involved as an essential part of the equation, as it must be. In most gay men's lives, contingent and unstable as they sometimes are with respect to normative sexual and power relations, it is the affirmation and exercise of this brave choice that breaks the vicious cycle of dependence. Saints are fully alive, fully self-determinant humans. Confessing, self-accepting gay men, men who witness to their own integrity and that of their gay brothers, can be saints in the making. Coming out, the mark of our baptism into the gay community, is often the first step on the voyage.

Third come the saints known as doctors. They form a distinct minority. There are only a handful of them, often the prominent male theologians of the early church, with even fewer women claiming the title. The most recent is Saint Thérèse of Lisieux, who, despite her very young age, was accorded the title in recognition of her exceptional and unique brand of spirituality known as "the little way," the idea that our relationship with God should be modeled on that of child to parent, and that grace is found in the most commonplace of life's daily moments and events. In order to be declared a Doctor of the Church — meaning "a teacher, someone learned" — an individual must have made a truly exceptional contribution to the formulation of the Christian truths, either from a mystical or a theological perspective. Doctors often stand as the giants among the saints, men and women whose influence or insights have been formative of Catholic thinking, and whose stature and charisma remain timeless.

Throughout gay history, a few individuals can lay legitimate claim to having been our learned men, our guides, our doctors. They may not all have chosen, at any given period, to affirm themselves as homosexual, but their sensibilities and insights as molders of the gay consciousness remain part and parcel — the crux — of who we are today. I think of the naked masculine glory and beauty of Michelangelo's works; of the tortured depths of Tchaikovsky's wild and haunting symphonies; of Walt Whitman and his robust poetic hymns to democratic comrades; of recently deceased Harry Hay and his early political organizing and Radical Faerie play; above all, of Oscar Wilde, the great and learned one, who earned for us the distinction of having an unvoiced love, and who claimed, for each of us, a collective identity for all of posterity. I think also of the lone Jesuit voice of John McNeill confronting his church for her failings to claim us as her children; of Troy Perry fearlessly affirming the special love of God for LGBT people, and then founding a church to prove it; of armed and dangerous philosopher Michel Foucault telling us that the power is always there, always ours to be picked up and deployed; of historian John Boswell reclaiming the faint though lost speech of gay Christianity. These have all been truly inspiring, formative voices, doctors and molders of spirit, mentors to generations present and to come.

It is from the hands and voices of such as these — our own martyrs, confessors, and doctors — that we have received the promise of our inheritance. Though some may want to call it idolatry, we can certainly reach out to those no longer with us, invoke their holy names and example in our prayers, bless their gifts with much gratitude and heartfelt thanksgiving. Gayness is not solely a function of sexual or affective preference; rather, being gay means understanding and appreciating the complex and subtle links binding us to our common birthright. Being gay is a choice in favor of some semblance of human solidarity, an intensely communal undertaking. Along the way, we need others to walk with us, to lighten the load, to point out the dangers. We always need those who have gone before. We always need our saints.

No doubt some canonized saints were homosexual, as were other holy men from the Judeo-Christian tradition. Biblical sources recount the love that existed between the future King David and his friend Jonathan, a love "more wonderful than the love of a woman." Intimate male friendships were once far more commonplace than in our own era, concerned as so many men are about not giving the impression that they are in any way sexually attracted to others of their gender. John Boswell has demonstrated quite eloquently that the early Christian religion made room for same-sex desire in the form of paired saints, partners in life and in death.[51] He cites the example of Saints Sergius and Bacchus, long venerated as patron saints of the military in the Eastern tradition. It has been generally accepted that they were, in actual fact, lovers. As is often the case with the stories and legends of other Christian soldier-saints, Sergius and Bacchus refused to sacrifice to the Roman gods. For this, they were humiliated by being paraded in public in women's clothing. They were separated and subjected to various forms of torture. When Sergius was losing heart, Bacchus, who had already been martyred by being flogged to death, appeared to him in a dream, encouraging him to persist by promising union with himself in the hereafter, rather than the usual heavenly reward of martyrdom. As Boswell so perceptively points out, this "was remarkable by the standards of the early church, privileging human affection in a way unparalleled during the first thousand years of Christianity."[52] For these gay saints, the significant other himself, the lover, became the ultimate prize to claim. His glorified body, rather than that of Jesus, was the reward for the witnessing.

Saint Aelred of Rievaulx, a British abbot from the twelfth century, is another holy man often claimed by gay men as one of their own.[53] A much-loved Cistercian monastic leader, it is said that he had many very close male friends during his lifetime, including a favorite monk in the abbey. He was a gentle guardian of souls and of his fellow monks. His classic devotional text, *On Spiritual Friendship,* praises male friendship, love among brothers, as an opportunity for growth in the spiritual life. At his death, legend has it that he was surrounded by his religious charges day and night, and that they exchanged words of endearment and affection. In his valuing of friendship between men as a means of attaining religious perfection, Aelred extols one of the core values of the gay community. Because many of us do not have the presumed luxury of traditional families or of marriage, friend-ships with other gay men, very often sexual at their source, occupy a significant and vitally necessary place in our lives. These close friends very often become an extended surrogate family, filling many of the same roles and needs. We celebrate, laugh, and drink with them; we also cry, fret, and hide with them. We may even, at times, choose to sleep with them. With this unique and potent mixture of affec-tion and erotic desire, new vistas for understanding and appreciating friendship as a rich and diversified source of spiritual communion open up. Saint Aelred of Rievaulx, loving shepherd to his brother monks, gentle father to his children, would no doubt have welcomed the possibilities.

What saints do is flaunt established conventions, whether cultural or specifically religious. Queer saints, male or female, do so with a touch of extravagance. I remember hearing and reading stories about female saints growing beards to make themselves less attractive to potential suitors, of male saints walking the streets of towns and vil-lages in drag as a way of practicing humiliation and self-effacement, of saints of both genders choosing to unite themselves to their mystical bridegroom through wildly enticing acts of sado-masochistic abne-gation. In such cases, gender enters a different realm. It becomes a shifting concept, more spiritual performance than biological essence: gender-bending, or rather gender-confusion, as a privileged and cre-ative means to the attainment of one's personal sanctity. Sometimes, when I see men in the process of transitioning to women, awkwardly dressed in ill-fitting female clothing, I think of the exceptional courage and commitment such acts require of the individual. Others no doubt laugh at them. What I see, sadly touching in their lopsided wigs, are persons of strength, integrity, and foresight. I am further reminded of those many chaste adolescent saints who were no doubt jeered by their peers as sissy boys and fops, less manly because they chose the unpopular path of sexual denial. How effeminate and unmanly they must have seemed to other men, yet how much more genuine and comfortable they must have been in their persons. Saints are manifestations of the truth. And if that truth is about same-sex desire or sexual difference, then all the more power to the queer saints, dead or alive.

Wanting to be a saint sets up an almost irreconcilable dynamic with respect to the broader culture, for saints tend not to be very popular or necessarily likeable. Saints are there to question, to confront us with our imperfections, to remind us of our sad everyday shortcomings, and, of course, that is partly why they are canonized. There is, of course, another reason for their being raised to the altars. Saints are intensely individualistic and selfish. Saints seek out their own path for the journey, and they follow it to the bitter end. Saints can claim to hear voices, see visions, perform miracles, and we believe and respect them for it. Saints are not quite human, or, if they are, it is a slightly more perfect form of humanness. Saints can be so irritating. Consider, therefore, the gay saint, the sexually deviant or marginal saint, and how much more annoying and irksome his "virtuous" life must seem. He upsets everything that is heterosexually normative and sacred: gender, family, marriage, children, career, love, and desire themselves. This is really not all that much different from female saints generally, whose challenges to patriarchal structures and expectations have certainly been equally brave and disturbing, if not more so.

Though it is unfortunately difficult to prove the historical existence of saints who may have been homosexual, statistically they had
to have existed. In the clerical classes from which so many saints are
drawn, there can be no doubt that among some of those declared
saints — and some, not — there were lovers of men, sodomites, from
popes all the way to the simple priest. I think of Leo X, the Refor-
mation pope who was reputed to be a suave *connoisseur* of Roman
rent boys. I think also of the bishops, abbots, and religious superiors
who have had their young favorites among their flocks. I think of
men from my own religious group, the Congregation of the Blessed
Sacrament, who no doubt lusted after us and each other, and probably all at once. These men may not all have been saintly, some far
from it, but they were men like me, men who found themselves
happiest and most fulfilled in the sensual company of others like
them. I praise and salute these exceptional men. They do not carry
the title of saint, but they were and are my saints, my holy men,
my virtuous, consecrated models. I see myself in the walled-up cell
with the two young Latvian Dominican monks. I see myself moving
delicately with them through their daily rituals of prayer and mortification. I feel myself touching them, their rough monastic habits
being pulled gently over soft, angelic skin. I want to commune with
their saintly and illuminated bodies, healed in all my spiritual imperfections. I died with them in that holy space forever caught in their
celestial glow.

I want to be a gay saint. I want to rush the heavenly throne pulling
behind me all the drag queens, hustlers, and queers whose only stain
is that of their boundless love.

Blessed gay saints and martyrs, of all times and of all places, shed your precious light and mercy upon us. We salute you for your courageous, exemplary lives. We hail your uncompromising and vibrant holiness. We are grateful for your protection. Stand with us in times good and bad, reaffirm us in our difficult choices, bless us in our gentle moments of grace. Blessed Matthew Shepard, martyr, safeguard us. Saints Sergius and Bacchus, show us the way of integrity and honor. Saint Aelred of Rievaulx, teach us the wonders of friendship. Jonathan and David, bless us. Nameless, loving monks of Riga, bless us. May we grow to be more like you every day. May we become the saints we are called to be. Amen.

THIRTEEN

The Lover and the Activist: Understanding Gay Male Sanctity

I WOULD LIKE TO PROPOSE a schema of sorts, a way of deepening our understanding of what male sanctity might mean for us as gay men at this time and in this place, and to do so by looking at the opposing ends of an open spectrum. These ends are by no means mutually exclusive, but rather complementary in their design. I suggest the ideal types of *the lover* and *the activist,* and I conjure up Saint John the Evangelist and Saint Thomas More, respectively, to fill them with their generous presence.

These are two formidable saints. One embodies total love and devotion; the other, conscience at its most enlightened and engaged. More importantly, each is an extension of the other: to love is to be engaged, and to be an activist implies that one loves someone or something. John the Evangelist — often depicted and understood as the beloved apostle of the gospels — was one of the first disciples of Jesus, the writer of an exceptional story of his life, a theologian, and, some would say, his lover. Thomas More emerged centuries later in Tudor England, trusted friend and chancellor of Henry VIII, a skilled diplomat and politician, who lost his head because he refused to bend his principles and go against his conscience, even for the king. I have always had a great deal of admiration for both men, for it seemed to me that they each modeled how one should choose to live life in the two realms of the private and the public: as a supplicant, friend, and lover; and as a committed though cautious citizen. As a paradigm for life, I believe such models can still guide us, and I propose them to gay men of today. Essentially, these two saints provide a context for the two sides of our identities, needing and supporting each other. As we know, the thin line between private and public remains illusory. All the more reason that we should learn to become activist-lovers, and, equally, lover-activists.

I came of age during the era of the Vietnam War, of draft dodgers, free love, and the civil rights struggle. Individual conscience was a big thing for us. We heard about it all the time, whether as a statement affirming cultural or generational difference, or as a strategy of political resistance. My hero was Daniel Berrigan, the American Jesuit priest and poet who, together with his brother Philip, burnt draft files as a way of protesting the war, and then evaded capture by the FBI for several months.[54] I also recall seeing the film about Thomas More, *A Man for All Seasons,* and it marked me. His life was one of those I read about during our spiritual reading sessions, and I recall writing a paper about him for a history course I was taking. More than anything else, Thomas More embodied the ability to walk with power, while remaining cautious and wary of its intentions, knowing when the line between principle and compromise has been crossed, and, ultimately, being able courageously to choose to say no. Berrigan and More exemplified, for me, what was most noble and audacious about a type of "engaged" and relevant Christianity then very fashionable, and no doubt quite motivating for someone of my generation. They each made or were making a difference for their time, and I wanted to do the same, partly out of some simplistic hero worship, but also because I could see no other way of leaving my mark. The times were intoxicating. There were the Kennedy brothers and Martin Luther King Jr., but there was also the fatherly Pope John XXIII, and I equally idolized him. His ideal, more geared to reform, was of an open and modern Catholicism. He has since been declared Blessed by the currently reigning pope, a well-deserved and momentous acknowledgment of his significance.

Saint John the Evangelist is the voice of the "In the beginning . . ." gospel, a text of splendid and delicate beauty, of words measured and melodious. He was also the apostle who placed his head on the chest of Jesus at the Last Supper, and some claim that he was one of the two present at the postresurrection Emmaus revelation. Growing up, for some reason, it never really crossed my mind that Jesus and John could have been lovers. The idea would have been foreign, if not anathema, to the Catholic circles in which I found myself, circles at once strangely orthodox and liberal, but unwilling or unable to broach such topics. They certainly would not tell you this in the seminary, where any suggestion of homoerotic attraction, though not expressly forbidden in words, was strangely silenced and therefore apparently nonexistent. Much later, I found the idea intriguing, though my ingrained childhood Catholicism had a hard time not being skeptical. It is, however, a beautiful image, a deep and touching affirmation of our central place as gay men in the heart of God. This relationship between the beloved apostle, John, and Jesus is one of the rare instances in scripture of same-sex attraction and desire. I can see why John would have been the chosen one. Often portrayed in iconography as younger, possessed of a fine and intelligent mind as his limpid gospel words bear witness, John must have touched the soul of Jesus, and claimed his body and heart.

The activist and the lover. Activist-lovers and lover-activists. Saint John, chosen favorite friend of the divine. Saint Thomas More, conscience speaking to abusive power. As gay men, we know both. As gay men, we have encountered the wondrous warmth of male love and care, and the deadening and violent hatred of normalized dominance. In our lives and loves, as in our engagements and politics, we see where we need friends to walk the way with us, and models to provide the cautionary voices. John the Evangelist: a man possessed, taken, fully in love, faithful to the end; Thomas More, a man of wisdom and discernment, contained, fearless unto death. Both are men of contemplation and action; men attentive and available to divine summonses, whether whispered or declaimed in a blinding clap of thunder. Saints can really only help on the journey here below; show us what some of the possibilities are; help us move ahead despite, or perhaps because of, the inevitable obstacles; point the way forward by the exemplary force of their own lives; in a word, encourage. That is why we need John and Thomas.

Top and Bottom Saints

Writing this book has been an odyssey. I have taken a look at a small selection of Catholic saints, and tried to read them as one might an encoded historical or ethnographic text, teasing the queer elements from the text, trying to "read out," or rather "read in," same-sex desire and affinity. I have argued that this process of "unpeeling" is both advantageous and necessary: the first, because it reclaims our proper religious legacy as gay men; the second, because it is an act of liberation and affirmation, both culturally and spiritually. Throughout, I have deliberately mixed together different words and images, borrowing quite freely and consciously from theology and queer theory simultaneously, making and stretching connections not obvious at first glance. I have cut and pasted, and even made gratuitous assumptions, far more times than might seem academically proper for a serious scholar of religion. I gladly confess that I have done all this with the firm intention of causing trouble: not to myself or to others, mind you, but to a hagiographic tradition that remains deaf to the bothersome complexities of human lives, ours and those of the saints themselves.

I feel I need to go even further, and I intend to be rather outrageous about it (and no doubt blasphemous, in the eyes of some). Let me therefore suggest that we can also choose to imagine "top" and "bottom" saints: saints you can visualize panting away with gusto in or on top of you; others, you would prefer they were squirming hungrily under you. You can be screwed by your saint, as much as you can screw him. I readily admit that the top/bottom "thing" (or is it another one of those endless postmodern debates?) is very much a question of personal taste, whether good or bad. One man's bottom can be another man's top, or vice versa (it's really all a question of basic acrobatics!), and I am not one to judge the respective merits of the best (or at least, the most convenient) resting place for the sad and homeless male organ. "Top" and "bottom" have as much to do with biology as they do with a given state of mind at any given time. More importantly, they are not simply sexual positions, but strategically meaningful erotic practices — discourses of desire and of the body — and that is how they need to be understood. How, and also with whom, I choose to position myself in bed (or wherever) are acts of consequence.

In a chapter entitled "Is There Sex in Heaven?" from *Queering Christ*, Robert E. Goss writes about the unique spiritual dimensions and pleasures of anal intercourse for gay men:

> Gay men find an effacement of the boundaries of self, an ecstatic disruption of self that Georges Battaile has linked to the heart of mysticism and eroticism. This *jouissance* ("pleasure in orgasm") in anal intercourse represents an important element in the spirituality of many gay males, for it effaces self-boundaries in a communion open to spiritual possibilities for gay men.
>
> Men lying joyfully on their backs with their feet ecstatically in the air or in a variety of receptive postures arouses fears among heterosexual men, but for gay men, it signifies receptivity, trust, intimacy, vulnerability, and spirituality. Anal sex carries profound human as well as spiritual meanings.

202

Penetrating another man or getting penetrated by another are powerful, intimate, and spiritual experiences.[55]

In *Out on Holy Ground*, I wrote:

This openness to a willful condition of receptivity in the sexual act is, I would argue, one of the distinguishing marks of gay male sexuality, something not always readily understood and accepted in a heterosexist, patriarchal culture. It also goes beyond the isolated sex act or our concomitant erotic choices. Our sense of self, and of our place in the world, I would suggest, is intimately tied up with our openness to passivity and to active receptivity. This represents a fundamentally spiritual attitude toward life.[56]

The spiritual experience is, at its heart, one of ravishment, of complete and total filling by a power greater than ourselves. Gay male sexuality, particularly the experience of being "the bottom" in anal intercourse, mirrors, in a very real physical way, at times painfully, this image of ravishment. As I give myself up to my partner, allowing him to penetrate one of the most intimate and sensual parts of my expectant body, to dominate and subjugate me with his own body and desires, I enter a sacred space of vulnerability, giving, and communion. In the intensity of this transcendent moment when I no longer belong to myself, I lose myself, only to attain a greater awareness and pleasure in the act of a selfless offering to the other. I move outside myself. I become the loving receptacle. As "the top," my experience is quantitatively different, but my gift is equally valuable. I possess and claim my partner, intensely offering him a comparable token of intimacy and deep human sharing. I give him pleasure. My desire becomes his. We are one being. I am the instrument of his self-transcendence, of his spiritual communion and illumination.

Together, we plunge into a realm of deeper and more satisfying intimacy. I become the medium of the sacred, a ravishment that moves in and through me, and into the willing and receptive body and soul of the man I claim. Such might be the beginnings of a gay theology of the anus.

When I name myself as a "top" or a "bottom" (and they *are* fluid categories), I am saying much more than how I would like to engage in sex on any particular occasion. I can be one or the other, or both, at different times, or simultaneously. Depending on the nature of the relationship, I can also choose to be one way for an extended period of time within that same relationship. I can choose to meld myself completely with the dominant man of my fantasy, let him subjugate my erotic desires, and receive quite willingly and eagerly his energy and seed. I can also quite happily be the reverse at some other time, or under different circumstances. Top and bottom imply contingent and fluid categories of sexual choice. Equally important, it could be argued that they denote certain existential attitudes, and that they hint at our particular proclivities with respect to the experience of life in general, and of being human. Though one needs to be cautious of reified binaries, these sexual choices simultaneously reveal and mimic who we are.

To speak of top and bottom saints implies a number of things: first, a reference to a general spiritual attitude; second, an erotic positioning with respect to same-sex desire; and third, a redefining of hagiographic devotion as a form of desire. The cult of saints, quite apart from any of its historical, cultural, or sociopolitical dimensions (and these are certainly important), is grounded, first and foremost, in the special type of rapport that is established and maintained between the believer and the saint in question. The devotion to saints is primarily a relational phenomenon, founded on a personal affinity between the devotee and his or her saint. This affinity can have its source in a variety of places, most often in the devotee's own life experience. The saint in question may have entered the devotee's life at some particularly critical or significant moment, or the perceived power and influence of the saint may have played a part in the fulfillment of some material or spiritual need. The saint may also be attractive because of his or her specific personality. There may be something exciting about their life work, their spirituality, their teachings, or their ability to serve as a model for me and for others. As has been hopefully amply demonstrated in these pages, saints appealed to me for two reasons: they made it possible to learn about same-sex desire, and they made a relationship with holy things and persons immediately and dramatically accessible to me.

Insofar as saints are the projection and the reflection of our hopes and fears with respect to our spiritual and physical longings — insofar as they become creative sites of an eroticized religious desire — they can be experienced as either top or bottom. Top saints are those by whom we want to be ravished. Bottom saints, we would prefer to penetrate. And sometimes, there are saints who elicit both kinds of feeling in us. I playfully suggest that Michael the Archangel, John the Baptist, Joseph, Paul, and Augustine, as well as the more elusive Francis Xavier and Peter Julian Eymard, are saints I would choose to have as tops. Sebastian, Tarcisius, the North American and Ugandan Martyrs, Dominic Savio and his boyish confreres, Francis of Assisi, and Damien of Molokai are bottom saints for me. Others come across as more ambiguous and unstable, crossing sexual boundaries: John the Evangelist, Thomas More, even, occasionally, Francis of Assisi, Sebastian, and Eymard. One saint I might change my mind about is Paul. He could use a good lesson in vulnerability. And in my weaker moments, I might see myself under Dominic Savio.

Such a listing is amusing, but it does reveal how saints can embody, for gay men, certain key notions of masculinity, and how this masculinity, in its fantasy versions, is so often equated with the active sexual partner. Michael, John the Baptist, Joseph (perhaps), Paul, and Augustine are manly saints. They dominate the imagery of saint-hood. They are popular and familiar, confident in their beliefs, and secure in their positions. Even the church itself considers them top saints; they continue to stand as the reference points for much of its theology and belief. Francis Xavier is a top because he must have been sexy, and Peter Julian Eymard for reasons having to do with his role as mentor. Other saints tend to be more feminized in their characters, more passive, more gentle or submissive, therefore bottoms. A num-ber of them have known martyrdom: Sebastian, Tarcisius, the Jesuit missionaries of North America, the Ugandan sodomite-saints. Then there is poor ostracized Damien of Molokai. Those saints like the an-drogynous Francis of Assisi, the virginal Dominic Savio and Aloysius Gonzaga, or the ambivalent beloved disciple can leave one puzzled and unsure, but you sense that they might welcome a little roughness. Thomas More remains a bit of an enigma, perhaps too principled for his own good. Gay saints are almost off-bounds, respect and adula-tion being strangely stronger than erotic impulse. As for the Christ figure, he invites a transgendered, highly equivocal response.

Sanctity is a fluid category, which is why one can so readily play with it. As gay men, we amuse ourselves with this game of categoriza-tion: Is he a top or a bottom? Or sometimes, we just think we know because we can sense it in some gesture or bearing of the body. Gay-ness is also a fluid state. We play with it nonstop. We fantasize about its possibilities. We adopt different positions sexually or, more often than not, only in our minds. Men elicit different responses from us. At times, they make us want to be theirs; at other times, they make us want them. On our knees in front of our favorite saint(s), we choose how we want to relate to the holy. Are we the top or the bottom? Do we want to be filled, or would we rather fill? How can we best enter into this state of transcendence? What position, finally, should I assume? The ideal is one of flexibility, as are sexually, I am fairly certain, the vast majority of gay men. At times, I need to be ravished by my saint or by my god, as by my man, because my soul and body crave it. Other moments, I need to seize and possess him, because he desires me that way. I am compelled to enter him so that I can find myself through my release into him.

Queer(ing) Devotional Practices

The unique personal rapport that the believer and the saint enjoy can also be the occasion for the acting out of a variety of devotional practices and strategies, some of which can be quite queer. Throughout these pages, I have been engaged in a process of "queering" hagiography. I have examined the lives and imagery of a limited number of male saints, and I have recast them as gay icons. My own life has served as one of the templates, but I have included elements borrowed freely from gay culture or from some broader theological or religious perspectives. As with any queering tactic, my intent has been to question and destabilize, to reframe the discourse of sanctity in a different and, for gay men at least, more meaningful and relevant context. I refuse to believe that we should content ourselves with the occasional crumbs of care and inclusiveness dropping from the church's institutional table. This table is a seductively empty mirage, one that is only designed to keep us on our appetite. As with that wonderful gospel story, we should go out to the lanes and highways, and bring to the table the outcasts and the disfigured, the emotionally scarred and the violently hurt. Make it our own table, if need be.

In the same way that feminists have refashioned God in the image and likeness of women, so we should color the face of God and other members of the celestial entourage with the brush of same-sex desire. I will gladly admit my Catholic bias. This obsession with saints and other such beings will no doubt impress (if not disturb) some as smacking of papist idolatry. Yet these individual saints are spiritually and culturally iconic, embodying within themselves, and in the stories and legends of their lives, the limits and possibilities of what it means to be fully human. We need them, almost as much as they need us, to give them life and relevance. The other part of my Catholic "bias" has to do, of course, with the uniquely homoerotic dimensions of Catholic clerical desire, of the things I may have learned to wish for and fantasize about during my seminary years. I certainly make no apology for this, for I believe this period of my life to be particularly rich and fertile in the emergence and formation of my archetypal universe. If seminary means "seed-plot," the place where one plants a seed or a germ, nourishing it so that it hopefully grows to full maturity, then my own time in such a hothouse (or what we then called a "house of formation") was fecund and positively teeming with unformed, unspoken desires. Such desires, I believe, are what saintly devotions are all about; gay saintly devotions, perhaps even more so.

In the title of the book, I bring two things together: sanctity and male desire. I am saying a number of things, and making a few unusual assumptions: that there is nothing aberrant between desiring men and being a saint; that one can be keenly devoted to saints and still want men; that attraction to saints and homoeroticism are synonymous, or at least not in complete opposition; and that devotion to saints can be understood and written about as a source of gay experience and knowledge, whether spiritual or, more broadly, cultural. My queering strategy is constructed around a counterinterpretation: that male saints generally, and certain types of male saints more specifically, can serve as sites of homoerotic attraction and affirmation. One can desire male saints; fall in love with them; make love to and with them (though perhaps more figuratively than in actuality); see them as heroes, friends, and partners; and finally, but by no means least, understand that male saints can be a terribly and shamelessly sexy lot, at least to our queer eyes. And therein lies the devilish difference. Our queer eyes fix the gaze, and they make the saint queer. They imagine his body, his eyes, his hands, and his penis. They make the links with our gay identity and with our gay culture. They name our desires for us: desires born of shame, but no longer; desires claimed and fulfilled; desires defiantly and eloquently subversive.

From this queer naming flow our queer devotional practices. What might these be? First, there is the taming of the saint, the slow and melodious flirtation in the dark, at prayer, the seduction of both the man and the forbidding theological construct. This is a time of sweet and delicate danger, a risky time of uncertain intimacy. Second comes the moment of grace and union, the occasion when love is declared, and the fluid is expelled in his honor, a point of familiar contact and desires met. We make the saint our own. We subjugate and claim him. Third, the instant of soothing whispers and of secrets shared, of desires spoken loud and proud. The confident time of boyfriends and other public lovers. Lastly, there is me, the lone author, sitting here on a cold winter morning, writing these words of love and affection about my own saints: a coming out with respect to religious and hagiographic fetishism; of how these beautiful, manly saints continue to inhabit my insides, gnaw at them, and fill them. A story of how they, in turn, have seduced me.

The queering of saints emerges from desire and pleasure — from the appetites of same-sex desire, and the pleasure of their obsessions. As I think back on what certain saints have meant to me, I see the uncertain and hazy contours of my own desires, not so much for them as religious figures, though that was certainly important, but because of how they embodied so alluringly the inseparability of the holy and the erotic. It was not a scandalous thing, this unexpected union of the two, but something natural and reasonable. It made sense. I was a piously obsessed boy, spending time on lazy summer afternoons in the coolness of my parish church, reading my missal or mumbling litanies to the good mother of Jesus. One of my very favorite parts of the liturgical year was the litany of the saints on Holy Saturday,

Easter eve. The melodic and repetitious chanting of the names sent shivers down my spine. It was a sensuous experience, voluptuous and enticing. As the names were intoned in the eerie silence of the semi-dark church, they were like those of absent yet ever present friends and lovers, fluttering and dancing in the gentle breeze. I was obsessed with Jesus, and in love with his saints. I pined away for one, yet fussed over the other. One remained mysteriously distant and unknowable; the others, sensuous and tactile, so eminently and desperately desirable. They were sexed; Jesus was above and beyond sex. I wanted to sleep with his saints, but only rest on the shoulder of Jesus.

That, of course, is what saints are supposed to do: bring us closer to the divine body and face. Their humanity should help us overcome ours, to deal with the distance separating us from his divinity. Not only were saints my heroes and models. They were also human bridges to the eternal, because the eternal was so aloof and untouchable in its sublime majesty. It was what I adored, not what I may have chosen to caress. Saints, on the other hand, were objects and persons waiting to be fondled, inviting my affectionate snuggles. That is how I wanted to see them. The pious queer boy that I was needed them to be this way, because he did not dare approach his God from a position of desire. That was way too frightening, much too scandalous and risky. He needed the intermediaries, the halfway men, to act as surrogates. He therefore obsessed about saints: their lives and legends, their virtues and sufferings, their bodies and deaths, their visions and ecstasies. Saints were different, just as he was in his queerness and his desires for other boys. And in their difference, he could hide his own.

The queering of devotional practices emanates from a dynamic encounter between the object of desire, whether the saint or the god, and its active subject, the queer devotee. Neither the object nor the subject is, in fact, ever really static. While each is different from the other, each also moves ever more resolutely, and of necessity, to a point of mutuality and need. Queering implies a stretching, at times a breaking, of the limits and bonds that circumscribe, from a theologically orthodox point of view, the proper ways of relating to the holy. Queering implies nothing less than receiving the saint's seed rather than bathing in his grace; penetrating or being penetrated by him rather than offering him empty tokens of worship and adoration. When we say "Pray for us," we mean "Make us yours." When we name him "Blessed" or "Saint," we are calling him "Baby" or "Sweetheart." That is in the nature of sanctity, to make us fall in love.

As I think about the lover and the activist, I summon forth and admire two images of the ever-faithful Saint Sebastian. One, a black-and-white photograph of gay Japanese writer Yukio Mishima, showing Mishima *as* Saint Sebastian, quite thin in a loincloth, tied to a tree, his hairy armpit and sides pierced by arrows. His gaze of beatific countenance seems fixed on some heavenly vision of homoerotic splendor. He is sexy and desirable, sinewy and delectable. The second icon, a Pierre et Gilles painted photograph from the late 1980s, reveals a far younger Arabic boy-martyr, beautiful and enticing in his innocent fairytale stare. Two arrows emerge from bloodless wounds, one in his chest, the other in his side, his hard body sculpted to the point of perfection. A thin white loincloth reveals the faint outline of an expectantly dormant organ. How I want to worship this glorious saint, these most desirable and beautiful men! On my knees, arms uplifted, I pray:

Saint Sebastian, lover and friend, make us yours;
Saint Sebastian, glory of ancient Rome, make us yours;
Saint Sebastian, soldier and martyr, make us yours;
Saint Sebastian, favorite of the emperor, make us yours;
Saint Sebastian, defender against plagues, make us yours;

Saint Sebastian, beautiful saint, make us yours;
Saint Sebastian, muse of artists, make us yours;
Saint Sebastian, icon of manly desire, make us yours;
Saint Sebastian, my sweetheart, make me yours.

To all the saints of my life and the men of my dreams, I pray:

Come, fill me with your love.
Come, fill me with your desires.
Come, fill me.
Come, make me a saint.

Notes

1. See Mark D. Jordan, *The Silence of Sodom: Homosexuality in Modern Catholicism* (Chicago: University of Chicago Press, 2000).
2. See *The Concise Oxford Dictionary*.
3. See Kenneth L. Woodward, *Making Saints: How the Catholic Church Determines Who Becomes a Saint, Who Doesn't, and Why* (New York: Simon and Schuster, 1990).
4. See the introduction to Stephen Wilson, ed., *Saints and Their Cults: Studies in Religious Sociology, Folklore, and History* (Cambridge: Cambridge University Press, 1983).
5. There is an extreme right-wing religious sect in Quebec known as *Les bérets blancs* (The White Berets). They are staunchly antiliberal and antisocialist. Their official newspaper is called *Michel* (Michael).
6. The marginality of American Catholics, until relatively recently, is a well-studied phenomenon. Groups that find themselves under cultural suspicion tend to adopt, as a matter of course, and for purposes of group solidarity and cohesion, a variety of coping strategies, one of which may be an overemphasis on the uniqueness and antisecularism of their religious heritage.
7. Freely translated from a French prayer card.
8. See the entry on Saint Joan of Arc in *Butler's Lives of the Saints — May: New Full Edition* (Collegeville, Minn.: Liturgical Press, 1996).
9. The title of the work is "Love Conquers All."
10. The symbolism of the struggle with the phallic angel as a form of erotic play should not be underestimated.
11. See Peter Brown, *The Cult of the Saints: Its Rise and Function in Latin Christianity* (Chicago: University of Chicago Press, 1981).
12. See Karim Ressouni-Demigneux, *Saint-Sébastien* (Paris: Éditions du Regard, 2000).
13. Thomas Waugh, *Hard to Imagine: Gay Male Eroticism in Photography and Film from Their Beginnings to Stonewall* (New York: Columbia University Press, 1996), 145.
14. See *Saint Sébastien dans l'histoire de l'art depuis le XVe siècle* (Paris: Éditions Jacques Damase, 1979), preface by François Le Targat.

15. See Yukio Mishima, *Confessions of a Mask* (New York: New Directions, 1958).

16. See *Saint Sébastien: rituels et figures* (Paris: Éditions de la Réunion des musées nationaux, 1993).

17. See John Francis Bloxam, "The Priest and the Acolyte," in Mark Mitchell and David Leavitt, eds., *Pages Passed from Hand to Hand: The Hidden Tradition of Homosexual Literature in English from 1748 to 1914* (New York: Houghton Mifflin Company, 1997), 263–74.

18. Donald Luc Boisvert, "Religion and Nationalism in Québec: The *Saint-Jean-Baptiste* Celebrations in Sociological Perspective" (Ph.D. diss., University of Ottawa, 1990), vi.

19. The reference is to a line in Oscar Wilde's "The Ballad of Reading Gaol."

20. See *http://www.templepriapus.org*.

21. Augustine, *Confessions* (London: Folio Society, 1993), 190.

22. Ibid., 55.

23. Ibid., 59.

24. Richard Hennessy, S.S.S., "Martyrs of Uganda," in *Eucharist* (New York: Blessed Sacrament Fathers and Brothers, 1968), July–August, 8.

25. Francis Marion, *New African Saints: The Twenty-Two Martyrs of Uganda* (Nairobi: St. Paul Publications, 1985), 16.

26. The following quotes and insights are taken from notes on a paper entitled "The Flames of Namugongo: Postcoloniality Meets Queer on African Soil?" by Ken Hamilton, presented at the meeting of the American Academy of Religion, Toronto, Canada, November 22, 2002.

27. See the entry on Saints Charles Lwanga and Companions (The Martyrs of Uganda) in *Butler's Lives of the Saints — June* (1997): 22.

28. The reference is in Jordan, *The Silence of Sodom*, 92–93.

29. See Mark D. Jordan, *The Invention of Sodomy in Christian Theology* (Chicago: University of Chicago Press, 1997), 10–28.

30. Ibid., 16, emphases mine.

31. See Guy Laflèche, *Les Saints martyrs canadiens*, vol. 1: *Histoire du mythe* (Laval, Quebec: Les Éditions du Singulier, 1988).

32. Roy M. Thompson, "Transition," in *Eucharist*, 15.

33. See David Nimmons, *The Soul beneath the Skin: The Unseen Hearts and Habits of Gay Men* (New York: St. Martin's Press, 2002).

34. Ibid., 10.

35. See Michael Bronski, *The Pleasure Principle: Sex, Backlash, and the Struggle for Gay Freedom* (New York: St. Martin's Press, 1998).

36. See Mark D. Jordan, *The Ethics of Sex* (Oxford: Blackwell Publishers, 2002), 155–72.

37. Saint John Bosco, *The Life of Saint Dominic Savio* (New Rochelle, N.Y.: Salesiana Publishers, 1996), 38–39.

38. On the history of masturbation as an illness, see Peter Lewis Allen, *The Wages of Sin: Sex and Disease, Past and Present* (Chicago: University of Chicago Press, 2000), 79–118.

39. See the entry on Blessed Damien De Veuster in *Butler's Lives of the Saints — April* (1999): 104–8.

40. Ibid., 105–6.

41. Luke 24:13–35.

42. Donald L. Boisvert, *Out on Holy Ground: Meditations on Gay Men's Spirituality* (Cleveland: Pilgrim Press, 2000), 97–98.

43. Robert E. Goss, *Queering Christ: Beyond Jesus Acted Up* (Cleveland: Pilgrim Press, 2002), 10.

44. Ibid., 139.

45. Ibid., chap. 6, "Christian Homodevotion to Jesus," 113–39.

46. Ibid., 80.

47. Leo Steinberg, *The Sexuality of Christ in Renaissance Art and in Modern Oblivion* (Chicago: University of Chicago Press, 1996), 15.

48. Ibid., 21–22.

49. See among Teilhard de Chardin's major works, *The Phenomenon of Man* and *The Divine Milieu.*

50. Perhaps the most powerful and informative of all is Moisés Kaufman's play *The Laramie Project.*

51. See John Boswell, *Same-Sex Unions in Premodern Europe* (New York: Villard Books, 1994).

52. Ibid., 151.

53. Goss, *Queering Christ,* 125–27.

54. See Daniel Berrigan, *To Dwell in Peace: An Autobiography* (San Francisco: Harper & Row Publishers, 1987).

55. Goss, *Queering Christ,* 79.

56. Boisvert, *Out on Holy Ground,* 116.

Index

pd $14 ²⁶
29 April 2005

Index